THE HISTORY OF THE CARERS' MOVEMENT

Tim Cook

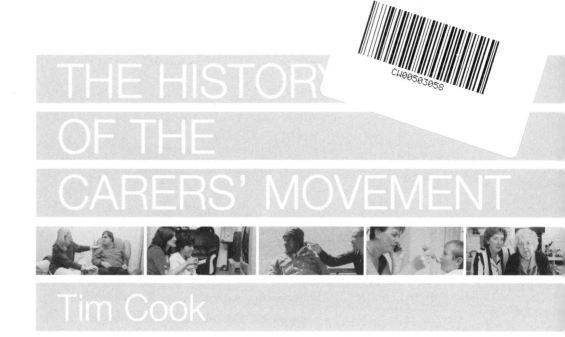

CARERS UK
the voice of carers

Published by Carers UK

20-25 Glasshouse Yard, London EC1A 4JT

© Carers UK 2007

ISBN 978-1-873747-36-0

Publication number UK7503

Registered in England and Wales as Carers National Association. Number 864097.

Registered charity number: 246329

Printed and bound in Great Britain by Biddles Ltd, King' sLynn, Norfolk

Contents

'The onset of a bout of depression would fetch us home for a while, but when no immediate recovery was forthcoming we would take ourselves off again while Dad was left to cope. Or care, as the phrase is nowadays. Dad was the carer. We cared, of course, but we still had lives to lead: Dad was retired – he had all the time in the world to care.'

(Alan Bennett, *Untold Stories*, Faber and Faber 2005 p.5)

Foreword

All of us have at some time been cared for by others and there will probably be times in our lives when others will rely on us for support. Even if we have not personally looked after someone with an illness or disability, it should not be too difficult to think of a relative or friend who has. Most people will provide support out of love or a sense of responsibility. Many will feel they have no other option. They probably won't even see themselves as a 'carer' but a 'parent', 'sibling', 'spouse' or 'friend'. But increasingly people are choosing to identify as 'carers' to seek support and recognition.

However providing such support, added to ongoing responsibilities, can be a huge strain on carers and without adequate support this can affect our health, our jobs, our finances and our social lives, as well as failing to meet the aspirations of those requiring such support to lead independent lives. An ageing population and increasing numbers of people needing support will inevitably bring social, economic and cultural strains that cannot and should not be borne by carers alone.

Seeking recognition has been a central and ongoing aim of the carers' movement. This book provides testimony to the central and crucial role unpaid carers play in society. Their success has been in turning what was once a private issue back in the 1960s into a cause that is firmly on the public agenda at the start of the 21st century.

Along the way, carers have battled for dignity, choice and equality, not just for themselves but for the people they support. A new alliance is forming between the disability and carers' movements around a shared agenda of independence and choice. Those supporting disabled people often share the experience of discrimination and disadvantage in their own right as they seek to balance work and family life. Important steps have been taken to tackle this discrimination, ensuring disabled people and increasingly carers are being included in the equalities agenda.

This is an exciting time in the history of the carers' movement. There is greater awareness of the critical role carers make to the well-being of our communities. At the Equality and Human Rights Commission, not only will these issues be high on our agenda but integral to the wider movement for equality and human rights.

Trevor Phillips
Chair, Equality and Human Rights Commission

Acknowledgements

Any history of carers now or in the future has to pay tribute to the foresight of Sandra Leventon who so scrupulously kept her papers from 1966 to 1999 which covered the two founding organisations of Carers UK and then wisely gave them to the Greater Manchester County Record Office. They are truly a mine of information both familiar and surprising.

I am very grateful to Francine Bates, Harry Marsh, Jill Pitkeathley, Judith Oliver and Imelda Redmond who gave up their time to be interviewed and so provided me with the personal perspective of those who were directly involved in some of the events described in these pages.

Professor Robert Woods gave me some very helpful demographic advice. Elizabeth East at the Carnegie United Kingdom Trust put me on the right track to find the earliest funding application from the Council and Shirley Otto very kindly unearthed all the material for me from the National Archives of Scotland. Chris Smith at Carers UK dealt most efficiently with all my telephone enquiries and Mara Normile and Tina Stiff at the City Parochial Foundation responded rapidly to my requests for old CPF reports and minutes relating to carers' organisations. Emily Holzhausen and Clare Woodford of Carers UK provided me with invaluable information about the most recent developments in the organisation.

To all of the above I give my sincere thanks.

ABOUT CARERS UK

Carers give so much to society yet as a consequence of caring, they experience ill health, poverty and discrimination.

Carers UK is an organisation of carers fighting to end this injustice. We will not stop until people recognise the true value of carers' contribution to society and carers get the practical, financial and emotional support they need.

Carers UK is here to improve carers' lives. We achieve this by

- Campaigning for the changes that make a real difference for carers
- Providing information and advice to carers about their rights and how to get support
- Training professionals who work with carers
- Mobilising carers and supporters to influence decision-makers
- Gathering hard evidence about what needs to change
- Transforming the understanding of caring so that carers are valued and not discriminated against.

ABOUT THE AUTHOR

Tim Cook worked in the voluntary sector from 1962 until his retirement from the City Parochial Foundation in 1998. He has continued to be actively involved in the sector chairing several merger committees, mentoring directors of charities and writing on a range of issues. He has always had a deep interest in the histories of voluntary organisations which he strongly believes are too often forgotten.

\

I
Introduction

The carers' movement is now in its fifth decade and by any objective criteria would be regarded as an outstanding success. Yet outside the movement itself the history of that success is little known. I was keen to write up that history for two reasons. First, the voluntary sector is poor at writing its histories except in the form of appeal literature or annual reports. Indeed, its archival material can disappear at a stroke – as I know personally – in, for example, the chaos of an office move. The carers' movement is blessed with an astonishingly full archive from 1963 to 1999 thanks to Sandra Leventon, a founder member of the first two carers' organisations, who assembled it and wisely gave it to the Greater Manchester County Record Office. As she said in 1999, her experience was that archives soon get 'lost or damaged' unless they are in official safe keeping. The catalogue alone runs to 229 pages. In such circumstances a history becomes possible and, one might say, is required. Second, the very success of the carers' movement needs to be understood in terms of why and how. It may well be that there are lessons for the voluntary sector developments of today. Certainly it is an instructive history when compared with other enterprises which began at the same time, in the 1960s, and which have seen their causes become increasingly difficult, the fields of addiction and penal reform being obvious examples. Some organisations have been as, if not more, successful, such as the Samaritans, which took its first call in 1953. It has continued to grow ever since, as well as stimulating the establishment of over a hundred other types of helplines.

This history is that of the movement, rather than a blow by blow account of the key organisations. The two may at times be indistinguishable, but I was aware of how easy it is to be drawn into the fascinating interplay of structures and personalities within and between organisations, and this is too familiar a territory to anyone who has ever worked in the voluntary sector. The main organisations in this history have had their darker times, but detailing that serves little purpose except when there are wider lessons to be learned or it impacts on the development of the movement as a whole. No charitable endeavour is all sweetness and light, and the carers' organisations are no exception.

This account is not an historical biography which can end quite neatly. The carers' movement is living, growing and developing. There is no end in sight, indeed it would be hard even to imagine what that end could possibly be: it is still an open book. Calling it a day is not on anyone's agenda. Whatever the future brings, I hope that this history may provide the platform for further accounts which will be able to root the work in the early pioneering years which inevitably come to seem even more like ancient history – not least the salaries the staff were paid. But, as I hope to show, the initial years of an organisation can set the style and tone for the future in ways that are often surprising. The past should not imprison a modern voluntary organisation, but equally the past should not be discounted. The records must be treasured. They will be read by few, but all need to be aware of them and from time to time they should see the light of day. This history is, I trust, a small contribution to that process of, if you like, recognition and education.

II
Before recognition

The 1973 edition of the two volume shorter OED makes no reference to 'carer'. In 1988, the Chambers Dictionary defines 'carer' as 'a person who takes responsibility for another, dependent person'. It was not until 1980 that the term carer first appeared in the literature of the founding carer body, The National Council for the Single Woman and her Dependants. As Jill Pitkeathley writes, 'we might be forgiven for thinking that caring had just been invented, that it sprang into being fully fledged, round about 1980' (*It's My Duty Isn't It*). The 'we' here is certainly the general public and ill informed professionals, for those thousands involved in caring knew only too well that caring was not new: that is, caring in the working modern definition current from the 1980s of a carer being 'someone whose life is in some way restricted by the need to to be responsible for the care of someone who is mentally ill, mentally handicapped, physically disabled or whose health is impaired by sickness or old age'. I will for ease of communication talk of carers at all times, but readers should be aware that it was not a term used before the 1980s and that the key initiative in this field did not happen until the mid 1960s. But what was happening to carers and caring before then?

Society has always needed to address the issue of the elderly no longer able easily to look after themselves. Even when the average life expectancy was low, there were still those who lived to a ripe old age. There is a reference in the Norwich census of 1570 to a widow, Alice

Coles, of 92. We can see the physical evidence today of monasteries, alms houses and workhouses, all of which played some part in caring for the elderly and sick. But families played the larger role.

Pat Thane, writing of the rural poor in 17th century England says: 'Poor relief authorities made every attempt to keep aged paupers living as active members within the community. This was cheaper than the expensive upkeep of institutions, more practicable in rural parishes, well adapted to custom, and was what older people preferred. Commonly parish offices paid neighbours, or even needy close relatives, to care for the mentally or physically sick, disabled and aged poor, thus often keeping the carers themselves off relief. Or relatives might pay the authorities to look after people in need. Carers were normally female but men might for example look after heavy or bedridden old men.' In 1796, Thomas Malthus wrote that the workhouse was not appropriate for older people 'who perhaps have been useful and respectable members of society and in their day 'have done the state some service". But the family was the safety net. A later study by Seebohm Rowntree showed that older people without children were more likely to end up in the workhouse. In reviewing past accounts of caring up to the 18th century, Thane concludes that 'a striking feature of all these accounts is their taken-for-granted assumption that mutual support between older and younger generations and, where necessary, sharing a household, was normal at all social levels, when circumstances required it'. There are certainly indications that unmarried children may have been the most important sources of assistance to the old.

It was the notion of the unmarried daughter as the caring relative that was to provide the impetus for the carers' movement in the 1960s. The concept of the 'dutiful daughter' had become a forceful one by the 19th century and, importantly, it impacted on the better off families as well as the poor. Had it just been the latter, it is interesting to speculate whether the carers' movement might have taken longer to develop, and in a different guise. But there were now articulate, educated and relatively well off single women being called upon to care for aged parents. Servants were no substitute. Thane quotes the conservative feminist Frances Power Cobbe as saying that it was an absolute obligation of daughters to care for their parents. Promising careers were put on hold or watered down. Helen Gladstone turned down the offer to become the first Principal of Royal Holloway College as she felt she was needed to support her father.

Some of the experiences which were to be so well publicised by the Council in the 1960s were evident long before. Sarah Acland was the only daughter of the Regius Professor of Medicine at Oxford, and when his wife died in 1878 Sarah went to be his dutiful daughter, secretary and housekeeper. She had that role for 22 years, so that on her father's death she was 60 and in poor health. Supported by her brothers (I should think so too!) she found a new role in philanthropic work. The tension of this dual role of dutiful daughter yet wanting something for oneself was succinctly expressed by Beatrice Webb in her autobiography: 'how to reconcile the rival pulls on time and energy, on the one hand, of family affection backed up by the Victorian code of feminine domesticity and on the other … an awakening desire for creative thought and literary expression.' In 1886 she had written in her diary of 'the narrow rut of Duty'. By no means all dutiful daughters felt like that, but on all of them the pressures were there and life was in some degree or other on hold.

The Beveridge Report was published on 1st December 1942. It was to lay the foundations of the Welfare State, but it contained next to nothing about the caring role. The role was still largely hidden, and those that had made it public were the relatively well off dutiful daughters who were not the targets of Beveridge. His welfare state was to tackle the five giants of Want, Disease, Ignorance, Squalor and Idleness. However, he had not been ignorant of the caring roles but on grounds of costs 'he had dropped plans to have full insurance for housewives, and benefits for those unable to work because they were caring for sick or aged relatives'. Nicholas Timmins comments that 'carers do not feature in the report, in part because if married women are not expected in the main to work, they are there for other 'vital duties". The unmarried woman carer is simply not on the agenda at all, even if only to dismiss her or her contribution. Invisibility was total.

The post war studies confirmed what anecdote, autobiographies and local studies had already demonstrated. For example the study by Elizabeth Roberts, *Women and Families: An oral history, 1940-1970*, showed that 'relatives were cared for because it was assumed that that was what one did'. There was even a fear of gossip and social disapproval if relatives were thought to be neglected. However, it has to be said that almost all studies were about old age, and the demands on carers were not prominently featured. Support for the elderly had always been provided in many ways. It was never simply a choice between the workhouse or being part of a loving caring family. There were countless variations in between, and still are in the 21st century. It could be complex, practically and emotionally. The carer's role as we now understand it was not fully articulated until the 1980s. But the emotional conflict of the position that people like Sarah Acland or Beatrice Webb (and of course many others) found themselves in was to be the driving force for the beginning of the carers' movement in the early 1960s. The Rev. Mary Webster, with whom it all began, echoed so much that had gone before, yet expressed it at a time that was ready to hear it. The 1960s evoke mixed feelings today, but for those of us who began our working lives in the voluntary sector in that decade it has much to commend it. The story of Mary Webster and the foundation of the National Council for the Single Woman and her Dependants are certainly reasons for commending it.

III

The start of the movement

The Rev. Mary Webster gave up her work as a Congregational minister in 1954 when she was 31 years of age. Her duty lay to care for her parents, her sister having married. Her father died in 1959 and her mother in 1964. It is clear that some two years before her mother's death, Mary Webster had been giving a great deal of thought to her predicament and the disadvantages, not least financial, that her sense of filial obligation and love had created for her. At this stage she had no idea at all whether hers was a rare situation or was all too common but never talked about. In January 1963 she burst upon the public with her proposal for helping unmarried women with dependants. There are no public records for any activity in 1962, though Mary Webster may have been sharing her ideas with close friends. The vigour with which activity began in 1963 suggests at the very least a determined New Year resolution. Even more important it shows her deep feeling that her situation – and indeed that of any others similarly placed – was simply not acceptable.

The charity she was to found, the National Council for the Single Woman and her Dependants (hereafter referred to as the Council), was not formally instituted until 18th November 1965, but much work was done before then. Even virtually on her own she was to lay down by implication much of the 'culture' that has been the hallmark of the movement for over 40 years. The culture of voluntary organisations can be remarkably persistent for good or ill – in this case for the good

– and is certainly one good reason why succeeding staff and committees should be aware of their history. So what was so striking about those earliest of days?

What is firstly so breath-taking is the sheer amount of publicity that Mary Webster generated in the early months of 1963. Ever since then the carers' movement has had a justifiable reputation for sound and extensive publicity. When Mary Webster began, she and her cause were unknown. However, what she had was a good story about an issue that had been almost totally hidden, presented by someone who was eminently sane and sensible but with a passionate vision to right a wrong. Reading the clippings today it is hard to believe this was one woman's work with no organisation behind her. Many well established charities would have been glad of half the publicity. Let me give just a taste of this and then look at the messages being conveyed.

In the first week of January 1963 there was a major article in the Guardian, *Single and Silent*, by May Abbott and an interview on the Home Service in the programme Home for the Day. Mary Webster was interviewed by Marjorie Anderson under the heading 'action stations'. Over the following months there were, for example, interviews and articles in the Methodist Recorder, Sheffield Telegraph, Daily Worker, Bradford Telegraph and Argus, Nottingham Evening News, Kentish Independent, Liverpool Daily Post and The Lady. Moreover, the publicity was not just a paragraph hidden on the inside pages. Incidentally she also recognised the telling phrase (a sound bite in today's language), describing single women caring at home as 'under house arrest'.

Secondly, what is impressive is the clarity of the message in the publicity. It was not just a story, as the BBC 'action stations' interview so clearly indicates. She wanted something to be done for a group of women who had been silent and hidden for far too long, for the newspaper coverage generated many letters of support so quickly she knew she was far from alone. She said 'I am loth to found just another new agency' but she saw no alternative. Interestingly, there had been an article in the Guardian in February 1963 on the Over Forty Association which dealt with the problems of 'unattached' women, be they single, deserted, divorced or widowed. Mary Webster wrote a follow up letter to the Guardian saying that the 'Over Forty Association is making an outstanding contribution to the field but much more needs to be done'. She could well have said that the single women she was concerned with were, on the contrary, all too attached, and therein lay the problem.

Thirdly, she had soon realised that a new organisation was needed and the idea of the Council was discussed in the articles and letters. The striking feature of the Council, as outlined by Mary Webster, was the combination of the immediately practical with the essential long term changes to ensure that the problem would not go on for ever. For Mary Webster it was a soluble problem though she recognised it 'will be with us for the next 20 to 30 years'. She envisaged from the earliest days that the Council should be working on a broad range of issues: research, advocacy, acting as a clearing house for information, being an advisory centre, setting up a trust fund providing interest free loans, tax reform, mortgages for single women, pilot schemes for accommodation for single women and their dependants, sitting-in services, extending home help services and creating a register of companions. It was her capacity and vision to combine, say, the need for tax reform with sitting-in services that was to serve the carers' movement so well thereafter.

Research was almost the bedrock of her work and that is the fourth characteristic that is so important and has remained so. Early in 1963 Mary Webster went to the LSE to obtain statistics to help her case, knowing that good personal stories alone would not, for example, bring about tax reform. At the LSE she met Nancy Seear, then a Reader in Personnel Management. Nancy Seear (Baroness Seear) was to be a key figure in the development of the Council and indeed the whole carers' movement until her death at 83 in 1997. Nancy Seear said that within five minutes of meeting Mary Webster 'I knew that she was someone quite exceptional'. In 1964, Mary Webster was working with Woolwich Council of Social Service (she lived in Eltham) and oversaw a survey in the Woolwich area to show the need of single women in positions similar to her own. They were many. Arguing your case from the data was always her way.

All the above might not have been so effective had not Mary Webster possessed an acute political instinct, a talent of hers surprisingly not highlighted in her obituaries. Following the publicity she had been receiving in the early months of 1963 Mary Webster called a meeting of interested women in July 1963. It was held at the House of Commons and sponsored by two MPs, Christopher Mayhew and Colin Turner. One MP who also attended was Miss Margaret Herbison, who was soon to be the Labour Minister for Social Security and was a key figure in the early debates on benefits for single women caring for dependants. One hundred women attended, coming from as far afield as Plymouth, Salisbury and Kettering. One MP said she had gone along expecting the usual 20 or 30 but had had to fight to get into the room. Letters of support were received from another 225 women. The meeting resolved to establish a Council and, more significantly, to draw the attention of Government and the opposition to the plight of single women and their dependants, stressing the need for speedy action. Political action was not to wait upon the lengthy processes of establishing a charity.

The meeting was rapidly followed up by a letter in August from Mary Webster to all her supporters and friends. It was on the notepaper of the National Association of Women's Clubs and it referred to the support the Council was now to receive from the Woolwich Council of Social Service. The letter reported on the July meeting and in particular gave details of the two resolutions. She stated that the second resolution had been to draw the attention of Government and Opposition 'to the difficulties that confront single women when they have to care for dependants, and urges that steps should be taken to consider and alleviate their difficulties through social policy and legislation, in particular they would request the immediate granting of the right to a housekeeper's allowance under the Income Tax Regulations'. Supporters were urged to send copies of the two resolutions to their MPs. There was now no turning back even though it would be two years before the Council would be legally formed. During these two years, 1964 and 1965, Mary Webster was both lobbying and laying the ground work for the formation of the Council.

In December 1963 Mary Webster wrote a memorandum making the case for a realistic income tax allowance for single women with caring responsibilities which was the basis of a deputation to the Chancellor of the Exchequer, Reginald Maudling, on March 10th 1964. Colin Turner MP led the deputation. Early supporters were also lobbying. In February 1964 Miss W Pringle wrote to her MP, Philip Holland, about the need to revise the National Insurance scheme to take account of the caring single woman. Maudling was just the first in a long line of Chancellors of the Exchequer who were to receive such deputations. It is worth quoting in full Mary Webster's account of this first deputation.

> 'On the 10th March I accompanied an all-party deputation of four MPs to interview the Chancellor of the Exchequer. We were again unfortunate in that our visit coincided with the Resale Price Maintenance debate in the chamber and the Chancellor himself could not be spared. However, we were interviewed by Mr

Alan Green, the Financial Secretary to the Treasury, and the Treasury officials. We felt we were given a kindly and sympathetic hearing. Mr Green began by informing us that we were too late for this year's budget (although this was the earliest date the Treasury had been able to give us!). However, this did mean that there was a freedom in the discussion. We were able to discuss fundamentals. You will find enclosed with this newsletter a copy of the memorandum which was presented to Mr Green on behalf of the Council for conveyance to the Chancellor of the Exchequer.

I myself was cheered by what must have seemed to others to be a very minor incident. Mr Green pointed out that tax concessions would not help the lowest income groups as on the whole they did not pay tax. I replied that we realised this, and were therefore asking for help from the National Assistance Board as well; in particular we were asking for 'an allowance for care and attention' for the elderly person in order to help with the family income. Mr Green remarked 'oh yes I have heard about that'. I almost felt like uttering a public cheer! Our words and memoranda are obviously penetrating through the various levels of administration somewhere.

We have since heard that the whole question is to be raised at the meeting of the Women's Consultative Council in the House, so we feel the progress is being made. We would again suggest that an approach should be made by all our members to their own MPs, if they have not already done so, and that these matters should be brought to the attention of all the candidates for the general election in the autumn.'

As an account of the first major lobbying by the carers' movement, the above is rich in its excitement, hope for the future and frustration: being told the meeting is too late for the budget when you had asked for a much earlier meeting is surely familiar to many in the voluntary sector.

As the account indicates, it was written in the newsletter to friends and supporters. By 1964 Mary Webster was sending out bi-monthly newsletters which were highly informative and must have been most encouraging to her readers. Sadly after numbers 2 and 3 there is a gap in the archives and they do not resume until number 25 in December 1968, with copies of only occasional issues thereafter. But the numbering shows that they were regularly produced. Numbers 2 and 3 alone provide a wealth of information indicating the concerns of the very early days.

On the lobbying front there had been a meeting with Lord Ilford at the National Assistance Board on January 10th 1964. This had been followed by addressing an all-party meeting of MPs on January 27th. A lot of lobbying was being undertaken. In newsletter number 2 in February 1964 Mary Webster writes that the members are receiving replies from MPs which are 'the mere repetition of a stereo-typed form' from within the Treasury, 'written by someone who has never experienced the problems with which we concerned at first hand at all'. It was because of this type of response that there was the drive to meet with the most senior Treasury officials.

Publicity continued, with two interviews on the BBC and an article in the Guardian on March 4th 1964. Each piece of publicity resulted in floods of letters, so much so that Mary Webster wrote in Newsletter number 3 'we find it impossible to believe now that anyone can say that there is no need for the Council'. This feeling was cemented by a meeting, an open forum, called in London on 6th March 1964 to discuss what services the Council should provide. The meeting was chaired by Miss Paula Byrne, the actress who played Dr Frances Whitney of the TV programme Emergency Ward 10 – the first but not the last example of getting 'names' engaged with the carers' movement. It was very well attended on a bitterly cold evening. A unanimous resolution was passed 'asking that our pattern of dependency should be recognised in the social and welfare administration'. The resolution was forwarded to the Chancellor of the Exchequer. Good practical publicity was also being developed. Supporters were asked to send in photographs of single women and dependants so that articles could be illustrated and the media made to see the personal side of it all.

As the geographical spread of attendance at early meetings had shown, as well as the letters, there was a real need for support, information and advice. In February, Glasgow formed the first local group and when later in July 1972 it contested its subscription to the national organisation, it claimed that Mary Webster had from the outset asked it to cover the whole of Scotland. Other local groups followed, as Mary Webster, working in and under the auspices of the Woolwich Council of Social Service, compiled the national card index, enabling single women to make contact with each other locally.

The services side was not being lost sight of, but the evidence of these years suggests that the main activities of the Council were to pilot schemes, make information available, and encourage groups to develop services locally rather than try to be a national service provider. Holidays for single caring women were manifestly a huge problem so in 1964 pilot schemes were to be tried out to see whether alternative caring arrangements could be made, allowing the single woman to go on holiday. Then in April 1964 members were informed of a report, *'Day Care Services for the Aged and Infirm in their Own Homes'* published by the National Council of Social Service. The office in Woolwich was running an embryonic advisory service, often building up their knowledge on the basis of information in the letters they received. For example, they were able to advise members that when an elderly dependant's sight failed, they could be registered as a blind person, giving access to other services. That there was this degree of unawareness of services indicates the isolation of the caring single woman.

All this activity was being funded by contributions to what was termed the sponsoring fund. Although there are no early figures available, by the time the Council was formally established it reported at its first full meeting on 15th December 1965 a bank balance of £357. On 31st December 1965 it had assets of £1,399.

With the legal establishment of the Council, Mary Webster was no longer a lone worker. The evidence of the work prior to December 1965 shows quite starkly the style and priorities of the movement, a culture which has stood the successors in good stead. With Mary Webster as Chair, the Council now began its work.

IV

The National Council for Single Women and her Dependants 1965-1982

Prior to December 1965 there had been an ad hoc committee, but on 18th November the twelve members of that committee formally resolved to establish the Council, which held its first Committee of Management on 15th December at 71 Rectory Place, Woolwich. The signatories to the resolution on 18th November included Nancy Seear, Sir Keith Joseph MP, William Hamling MP (Woolwich West) and of course Mary Webster. In this part of the book I want to discuss those 17 years, not on a year by year basis but by following up the themes that Mary Webster had previously articulated. 1982 might be viewed as the end of one era, as in that year the Council changed its name and widened its brief. Perhaps more significantly it witnessed the creation of a new 'rival' organisation, the Association of Carers, whose first AGM was on 30th October 1982.

Mary Webster died in 1969 at the age of 46, and as Founder was therefore not able to chair and shape the Council for more than four years. It therefore becomes particularly interesting to see how far her legacy was sustained and the culture, which she so firmly established, retained.

Before looking at the work in a thematic way I want to mention four elements which form the backdrop to what follows, together with a consideration of the first grant applications the Council made in 1966-7 where the role of Sir Keith Joseph, a founder committee member, was critically important.

The first is that in all the campaigning and headline catching work, the Council never lost sight of the individual single women struggling against injustice. It was not an organisation with a caseload but when roused it could rally all its forces to help an individual. In the newsletter of June 1972 the circumstances of one Miss Dorothy Pointon were highlighted. She was 51 and had lived in the family home in Sevenoaks for 46 years, caring for many years for her parents who had recently died. Sevenoaks Rural District Council had asked her to leave the house on 13th September 1972. She now shared the house with her brother, aged 40. The Council was outraged and asked through its newsletter that members write to the RDC. This they did in their hundreds. I would have liked to have been a fly on the wall that week in the quiet offices of the Sevenoaks RDC! By August the RDC had offered a lease to Miss Pointon's brother, which the Council said was inadequate as on his death she was still liable to eviction. The saga continued but the files do not record the final outcome. It clearly shows, however, the challenges still facing the Council's members and its willingness as an organisation to take up the fight for an individual.

The second is the narrow focus that the Council maintained, namely its concern with the plight of caring single women. One might say that the case of Miss Pointon above justified that stance. A broader argument in support of the Council's position is that organisations can easily lose their way if they adopt too wide a brief. There is strength in a really concentrated constituency. I remember being criticised, when in 1966 I started a hostel for homeless alcoholics, that we ought to be doing more in the way of prevention and helping less damaged people. Forty years on that, rightly, is what the charity I helped to start is doing, just as the successor organisation to the Council has a much wider remit. In the beginning, the Council stuck to its guns. In 1967 it defined the single woman as over 25 and never married. Widows were not included. Interestingly in 1967 fundraisers for the Council said the charity was being confused with the unmarried mother and her child, and asked if 'infirm' could be put into the name. The Council asked the Charity Commission for permission to do this but was advised against it.

A third key event to note is the appointment of the first Director, Roxanne Arnold, in 1967. She was to hold that post until her retirement in August 1975. Hers was perhaps an unusual appointment for the radical 1960s, but it demonstrated the way the Council wanted to go and the commitment to the founder's long term vision. Miss Arnold was 61, a barrister who had been manager of a trustee department of a merchant bank in the City. She was involved with a number of women's organisations, had led parliamentary delegations and assisted in drafting suggestions for legislation. When she retired, *The Guardian* profiled her on August 21st 1975 and described her as 'a tough, practical, unsentimental campaigner with impressive legal and financial aptitudes and an ability for exerting precise pressure on the right people'. She was clearly a worthy successor to Mary Webster and their combination as Chair and Director for two years must have been awesome. She also bequeathed to her successors a track record and style that she would, I am sure, recognise as still very much in evidence.

Lastly, whilst the single women caring for dependants were the driving force of the charity, their situation was known to a far wider constituency: families, friends and neighbours. People who were not members became heavily committed to the Council and one often wondered why. In 1966 Dame Flora Robson, the very distinguished actress, agreed to become the Council's president and was active with appeals on the Council's behalf. In the newsletter of December 1975 the factors behind her involvement became clear. She wrote as follows:

> 'My dear eldest sister, Lila, died in October aged 82, the 'ideal single woman' who had none of the benefits that we have worked so hard to get for our members. There were seven of us and Lila left school at 14 years of age as mother had a serious operation. Lila mothered us all, and the household management was in her capable hands. Her beloved Cameron Highlander was killed in the last German rush in 1918. She never wanted anyone else. Mother always needed her care, and there was a two year old nephew, David, whose mother had died, that she brought up with love and wisdom. She managed all father's money when he retired, and was a better expert on finance than I ever was, or the bank.'

It is little wonder that, as President, Flora Robson showed such insight and commitment. I am sure this kind of experience was shared by many of those who gave time and support to the Council, and what a strength it would have been for the charity.

An influential and active figure in the Council from the outset was Sir Keith Joseph MP, who had been a Cabinet Minister in the Conservative Government until the election of 1964 and was then Shadow Minister for Labour. He became a Cabinet Minister again in 1970. Sir Keith's involvement was to prove a vital factor in helping to secure the Council's first grant from the Carnegie United Kingdom Trust in 1967. Given the importance of that grant, the story of its application is well worth telling.

The Council had been unsuccessful in applying to the City Parochial Foundation in October 1966, when it had applied for a grant of £50,000 over five years to cover the costs of a welfare worker in London to help single women in necessitous circumstances. A similar application to the Gulbenkian Foundation also failed. Correspondence now began with Carnegie, which immediately gave £500 for office equipment. However, its Trustees felt that the Council's plans needed to be more moderate and at a sub-committee meeting in December 1966 indicated that a grant of £5,000 a year for five years 'might be contemplated if it could be constructively used'. By this stage it had also become clear that the Carnegie Trustees were more concerned about the Council's general needs than the special requirements of a local service. The Secretary of the Trust, David Lowe, went to London to meet with Mary Webster and two committee members, one of whom was Sir Keith Joseph. It was now made clear to the Council that a grant of £50,000 was not possible, and that even a lower grant would be dependent on the Council indicating how it would raise the balance, given it was stating that it needed £12,000 to operate, which included the salary of a general secretary.

On 7th February 1967 Sir Keith Joseph wrote an absolutely critical letter to David Lowe. In it he said that Mrs Sally Oppenheim had agreed to chair a small finance committee and she and Sir Keith had committed themselves to raise £7,000 a year to match any grant that might be given. He also said that a small executive committee would now be established comprising 'Mary Webster, Miss Seears, Mrs Oppenheim, William Hamling MP (to keep the party balance), an honorary treasurer and I'. On 1st March 1967 the Community Services Sub-Committee of the Carnegie Trust approved a grant of £25,000 over five years on a diminishing scale of £7,000, £6,000, £5,000, £4,000 and £3,000 a year. The minute noted that the 'initiative taken by Sir Keith Joseph inspired greater confidence in this young organisation'. It hardly needs to be said that Sir Keith's fundraising efforts over the coming years were always successful. The City Parochial Foundation was to give the Council a grant of £25,000 over five years in October 1971.

Until 1970 and his return to government Sir Keith was very actively involved in the Council's work. He was not just a name on the notepaper. Without his contacts and fund raising abilities the Council's early years would unquestionably have been much more difficult, and who is to know how it would have turned out if funds had not been secured from such a reputable source as Carnegie, especially given Mary Webster's early death in 1969. Interestingly, the authoritative biography of Sir Keith by Andrew Denham and Mark Garnett published in 2001 (he never wrote an autobiography) makes no reference at all to his work with the Council and very little to his charitable work in general. The authors do write that 'the solid evidence of his early parliamentary career proved that he sympathized deeply with the *genteel* poor, particularly those who were elderly'. But how Sir Keith actually met up with Mary Webster and became so committed to the Council remains a mystery, and a novelist's imagination may be needed to provide the answer.

A final fascinating sting in the tale of the Carnegie grant came in March 1967 when David Lowe, following two visits to the Council's offices, felt compelled to write about the quality of the furniture at the Council. He felt that the tables and chairs were reminiscent of 'café furniture and I hope you may feel you could spend some of the Trust's money on something of better quality'. Visits from funders are always full of surprises.

Turning now to the key themes for this significant period in the development of the carers' movement, I have to begin with campaigning and lobbying.

CAMPAIGNING AND LOBBYING

Accounts of the Council to date have rightly focussed on its outstanding successes in securing the Dependent Relative's Tax

Allowance in 1967, the Attendance Allowance in 1971 and the Invalid Care Allowance in 1976. These were certainly milestones, but there were many other similar issues raised by the Council which showed how important they regarded 'penetrating the administration' and indeed government with their 'words and memoranda'. For example, in October 1966 there was a deputation to the Financial Secretary to the Treasury concerning selective employment tax, arguing that changes were needed to avoid hardship in households with caring single women. It was a complex issue and led to a working party on taxation within the Council. This may well have been one of the factors that influenced the type of person the Council was soon to decide to seek for its first Director.

What is striking about their campaigning is how they engaged with other organisations, tackled any issue of concern to their constituency, were well prepared as a Council to investigate issues and were able to raise the general cause in parliamentary debates whilst having deputations on very specific matters. Let me illustrate these features.

The proposal for Dependant Relative's Tax Allowance had the support of 33 organisations. In 1969 a letter to the Treasury concerning tax relief for the care of the elderly and infirm was supported by 10 organisations including the Association of Social Workers, Mothers Union, Iona Community and the Federation of Soroptimist Clubs of GB and Ireland. A similar letter to the Treasury in 1971 had 27 supporting organisations, with 'others to follow', and this list included the Electrical Association of Women, Over Forty Association, Association of Hospital Matrons and Women's Farm and Garden Association. The term 'networking' never appears in the archives but that was the activity that underpinned much of the campaigning.

No relevant issue escaped the attention of the Council and again they engaged with others. In 1967 the Council discussed a recent CBI report on the employment of women which had advocated the extension of community services to minimise the difficulties of caring for the elderly. The Council proposed to ask the Minister of Housing and Local Government whether he would reconsider, as part of community services, issuing a circular to local housing authorities requesting them to include in housing plans sheltered housing for single women and dependants, or make provision for the latter with separate bedrooms for single women and dependants. In 1968 the Council liaised with the Child Poverty Action Group over prescription charges, arguing that any exemptions should include single women who had given up work to look after infirm or elderly dependants. Again, in 1968, the Council raised the question of telephone charges for the installation of phones for the elderly or disabled, living alone or alone for considerable periods. Sir Keith Joseph agreed to pursue the matter. In 1972 there had been a Family Law report to which the Council had submitted a memorandum urging provision for a daughter who has cared for parents to have the right to stay in the family home for life. Over 20 years later Jill Pitkeathley, Director of Carers National Association said of CNA's work: 'one thing that can be said of us: we have never missed an opportunity. Where the opportunity has presented itself, we've been there.' With every justification the Director of the Council could have said exactly the same in the 1970s.

The Council was far sighted in realising that matters of concern in the social policy arena would always require study before any lobbying could take place, and might also arise unexpectedly. It therefore quickly established a system of working parties which were ready and waiting when action was needed. The first of these was on tax and was constituted in 1966. It was added to in 1968 with standing working parties on housing, employment and social security and welfare services. Mervyn Pike MP (a talented MP from my home constituency) was the convenor of the last. The active volunteers were all in place before the campaign had begun.

Lastly, we should reflect on the general political lobbying and the particular campaigns. The former kept the cause in front of the politicians.

On 13th March 1967 William Hamling MP, a committee member of the Council and its Chair from 1969 to 1974, introduced a Private Members' motion in the House of Commons which was debated and carried. It was 'that this House notes the burden of maintaining dependent relatives, usually elderly parents, borne by thousands of single women, and that in carrying out a filial duty the daughter is performing a service which otherwise would have to be undertaken by social security and public welfare services; that this frequently involves many years of financial and physical strain; calls upon Her Majesty's Government to take early action to lighten these burdens by providing new social security benefits, and urges welfare and housing authorities locally to assist single women in this situation with such help that they can go on caring for their relatives at home without undue stress'. At the end of the debate Miss Margaret Herbison, Minister of Social Security, said she was certain that Mary Webster had highlighted one of the real social problems 'in our country today'. Then on 24th July 1970 James Kilfedder MP introduced a debate on the situation of single women and their dependants. This kind of parliamentary attention allied to the very specific campaigns is impressive and would be the envy of many voluntary organisations today.

What is especially intriguing in these early days is how soon the Council raised the issue of the savings to the state that were made by the caring carried out by single women. On 4th December 1967, William Hamling MP asked the Minister of Social Security what steps she would take to provide social security benefits for single women caring for dependent relatives who are 'saving the state about 15 to 20 pounds a week and it would be a liability on the state if they were not taking care of their dependants in this way'. Mr Loughlin, Joint Parliamentary Secretary to the Minister of Social Security, replied 'I agree there is a saving to the state, but I think the best way of dealing with it is to have the review we are now undertaking'. He went on to say that it might be best to pay the supplementary benefit to the person who was disabled rather than the person caring for them.

When campaigning for the Invalid Care Allowance (ICA) was underway (see below) the Council produced a report, *The Costs of Caring*, which showed according to the DHSS the annual cost of keeping an old person in an institution was £1,500 a year and that a GP said it was £5,000 a year in a hospital geriatric ward. The ICA would be £360 a year. The savings to the state of family caring were not further followed up until 1988 with the publication of the study, The Forgotten Army, by the Family Policy Studies Centre.

The Council's success with its lobbying for the Dependant Relative's Tax Allowance, the Attendance Allowance and the Invalid Care Allowance is now truly part of history. The first of these has in fact now been abolished. A few comments are however worth making about all three issues.

In the 1967 budget the Chancellor, James Callaghan, increased the Dependant Relative's Tax Allowance from £75 to £100 and made it applicable to single women as well as widows, divorced and separated women. The Council saw this as recognition for the first time of single women as a category in their own right as well as the establishment of the principle of relief for those who care 'single-handed'. The Treasury had also agreed to consider further representation from the Council on related concerns. The Council's minutes of May 11th 1967 were clear that all this had been achieved as a 'result of the direct work and advocacy of the Council'.

The Attendance Allowance for those needing constant care at home was introduced in 1971. One history of the welfare state seems to attribute its creation to the work of the Disablement Income Group, though this body had had a representative on the Council since 1966. Whatever the historical niceties the Council had been pressing for this benefit since 1967. A deputation of five members had met with Miss Herbison in 1967 to argue for an attendance allowance. The minister's response is interesting. She said that the proposal for an attendance allowance was not acceptable because others besides single women would merit the allowance, for example husbands whose wives were infirm. She did, however, say that though she could make no promises she would consider the matter further, but said resources and personnel were limited. She went on to say that the Ministry would pay Class Three National Insurance stamps for a person who had to give up work to look after elderly dependants. The Ministry was also willing to make discretionary payments in supplementary benefits to contribute towards the cost of care and attention of an elderly person. She expressed her willingness to receive a further deputation if alternative proposals were produced. This seems at this distance to be a clear message that she was taken with the case being put by the Council and that it was really knocking on an open door. Even so it was four years before the Allowance was finally introduced. However, when the National Insurance and Superannuation Bill was introduced in 1970 the Council was in a strong position to make important, detailed and humane recommendations about the procedures for claiming the Attendance Allowance.

The Council had soon realised that immediate results in the field of social security benefits were never likely. The fight for the ICA also showed the need to have a long-term perspective. In the summer of 1973 the Council was informed that the DHSS was preparing a report on social security provision and it was determined that its submission would be in by the end of 1973. The core of its submission from its own social security working party was to be the proposal for an ICA for those compelled to give up work in order to care for elderly dependants. This should be £7.35p a week, equal to the flat rate unemployment benefit. The allowance should not be dependent on contributions and the test for eligibility should be a medical certificate. There was also to be a request for Class One insurance credit for those having to give up work to undertake home care. Publicity for the Council's submission was to be planned. I shall discuss publicity in more detail below. In terms of tactics, it is fascinating to note that the Council resolved to find out from Sir Keith Joseph, the Secretary of State for the DHSS, the name of the officer responsible for the DHSS report, so that direct contact might be established. The Council was fortunate indeed that one of its founder members had been Sir Keith Joseph. The new allowance was not introduced until 1976 but the Council's work in 1973 proved to be essential.

Allied to all the Council's campaign work was its close attention to publicity and research.

PUBLICITY

What is most remarkable about the Council's approach to publicity is that from the outset it hired a professional agency, at a cost of upwards of £1,000 a year, to do this work. This was a far-sighted decision in that it demonstrated the priority the Council was giving to achieve lasting change so that, for example, as noted above, the Council's tactics with regard to its ICA proposals were to publicise them widely. To be effective, that had to be done with professional assistance and Group Seventy was engaged on this as on many other occasions.

In October 1969 there was a television film on the lives of four single women and their roles as carers. Group Seventy organised the publicity, resulting in many radio and TV interviews. Such activity also fed into fundraising appeals of which the annual appeal was especially important. Lists of companies or key constituencies such as female barristers would be provided. The treasurer of the Council, CN Lippard, is perhaps an unsung hero, for many treasurers might have balked at this type of expenditure when the income was far from secure. The Council from the outset saw the value in publicity and worked hard at it. In 1966 it ordered 10,000 reprints of a Times article (16th June 1966) entitled *Sympathy and Help for the Single Woman with Dependants*. Again, a bold move financially. History has shown the wisdom of this approach.

One of the Council's most imaginative pieces of publicity was to launch in 1969 a National Dependants Week, an event which under a different name (Carers' Week) continues to this day. Such a week provided opportunities both nationally and locally for publicity and debate. In the 1970 week, for example, a report was launched entitled *The Cost to a Single Woman of Caring for an Elderly Dependant*, written by Miss Eoleen Cole. For the then 15 local branches, this was invaluable material to discuss and give to the local press. In 1972 another report by Miss Cole was used; this time it was on the workings of the Attendance Allowance. Such weeks were invariably described in Council minutes as 'a great success'.

RESEARCH

From the earliest days, the Council was always concerned to undertake or stimulate research so that it had evidence for its submissions and statements. Certainly publicity and campaigning are greatly assisted by data.

At the third meeting of the Council's committee in March 1966, Nancy Seear proposed that the LSE should 'umbrella our research' and that she would look into it. This approach did not bear fruit, nor did a number of funding applications for research grants. This did not, however, prevent research being undertaken or encouraged. The most critical fact of all was surely the number of single women staying at home caring for elderly dependants, and the exact figure here is hard to pin down.

In a review of its first ten years, the Council said that the 1966 census showed there were 310,000 single women living with parents over retirement age, which does not, of course, mean they were caring for them. In *The Wages of Caring* (1974) the figure of 308,000 single women in the caring role was given. In a funding application to the City Parochial Foundation in 1971 it was estimated that there were 250,000 single women caring for elderly dependants. The application also said that the Inland Revenue reported there were over 600,000 single persons claiming the income tax Dependent Relative's Allowance, but that does not include those not paying tax nor does it show how many of that number are single women or where they are living. In 1971 there were 50,000 persons claiming the new Attendance Allowance. There was never a challenge to the total figure and in fact there was an acceptance that 250,000 to 300,000 was a credible number. To some extent the exact number was less important than the Council's ability to demonstrate the problems facing the single women in their caring role.

Just as with its publicity the Council used professional help, so it did with research. For many of its surveys and reports it engaged MAS Survey Research Ltd, which meant more authoritative research findings and more substantial publications – they were not just cyclo-styled sheets, not uncommon with many voluntary organisations at that time! In-house surveys were still undertaken, such as in 1966 the holiday questionnaire to 85 members to discover what were the factors preventing the single woman taking holidays. Significant reports included *Single Women Talking* (1970), *The Wages of Caring* (1974), *Conflict in Caring* (undated) and *The Faces of Caring* (1984).

In its 1971 funding application to the City Parochial Foundation, the Council drew on its surveys to describe the incidence of poverty in the families with which it was concerned.

> 'The surveys have indicated that the ages of the elderly relatives cared for at home are preponderantly between 75 and 95 years, and the ages of the single women when they give up work to care for them are usually between 45 and 55 years. The periods of care extend from one year to 25 years. Financial help is called for most frequently to meet the costs of the heating needed to keep the elderly person warm. The next demand comes at the point when the harassed single woman has to cut down her expenditure on giving up her job, or on the loss of her parents' pension on their death. Lastly, when the period of caring ceases the single woman's health is often impaired and her skills lost and she will be in need of a period of rest and rehabilitation which she cannot afford. Funds to alleviate these needs are virtually outside the scope of statutory and voluntary organisations to provide.'

By 1977 international activity was on the agenda when the then Director, Miss Heather McKenzie, went to Australia to advise its Government on its restructured caring scheme. International research was being undertaken into the economic and social value of caring for the elderly in the home environment.

A publication that was neither research nor immediate publicity but showed imagination was an anthology of writings from ancient Greece onwards which touched on the whole issue of the caring single woman, entitled *Feminine Singular*, and published by Femina in 1974. The Council was rightly concerned about the costs but went ahead partly supported by individual member contributions led by Nancy Seear. The book sold well and all costs were recovered. Apart from the archive copy it would be interesting to know whether any other copies exist out there.

As the funding application quoted above shows, the Council did not lose sight of the need for services for single women and their elderly dependants.

SERVICES

Direct services require staff. In 1968 the Council's staffing consisted of a Director, Deputy Director, Copy Typist, Book-keeper and Assistant. In 1970 it was broadly the same. Given the level of activity already described it is not surprising that the national organisation was not running, for example, a helpline. Whilst it always sought to respond to letters seeking advice and realised there was a need for a general advisory service, it believed it could be most effective through advice, support and information to its local groups which numbered 48 by 1979. Even so, by 1982 it was receiving 12,000 queries a year. Information, for example, about short stay homes for the elderly would be circulated to all the local groups and individual members. There were accounts that some local sitting services were very successful. But it is worth noting that in the Council's minutes there are virtually no figures relating to this kind of activity. It was obviously vital to the heart of the organisation, but the long term changes being sought through lobbying were the priority. Members, judging by their commitment to the campaigns, accepted this approach.

There were two areas where more hands-on work was undertaken, and both gave the Council difficulties. One was in housing and the other was in the appointment of liaison officers to work in support of the branches.

The Council had from the outset wanted to set up sheltered housing for the single woman and her elderly dependant together. An enormous amount of effort was spent in discussions with local authorities and housing associations to explore opportunities to make this provision, starting in 1968. It was in fact not until 1984 that the first two schemes were opened in North London and Leeds. Yet within two months the Director was reporting to the Council that 'despite strenuous efforts, single women carers are not coming forward to take up tenancies'. The situation improved slightly but the financial burden was too heavy for the Council and the schemes were soon handed over to the management of experienced housing associations.

The growth of branches to 48 in 1979 led the Council to find funding for the appointment of four part-time regional liaison officers who were to make the local groups more effective, not least by making more financial benefits and supportive services available for local single women carers. Trusts and the DHSS funded these posts initially. Funding became more difficult and, faced with an overall deficit in 1984, the posts were terminated as at 31st December 1984, though all post holders were past retirement age.

Services were provided, but what lives on in reality and not simply the folk memory is the campaigning and lobbying allied to the publicity. It was the very success of this work that led the Council in 1980 to consider broadening the scope of its work. However, some of the older founder members, though not all, believed that the job had now been done.

A NEW CHARITY

At its meeting on November 8th 1979 it was reported that because of 'extensive interest' in the problems of caring by research bodies, voluntary and statutory organisations 'it may be prudent for the

Council to broaden the concept of its work and it was determined that a paper on this projected policy should be prepared, outlining the reasons for doing so and the implications of such a policy if adopted administratively'. This was discussed during 1980. There were good practical reasons for a change; for example, the statutory authorities would not limit their concern for carers to unmarried women. Some members were saying that the disadvantages of the earlier years no longer existed. 'The Council is no longer necessary.' By September it was reported that the Charity Commission would be unlikely to approve a widening of the objects and that a new charity embracing all single handed carers might be the way forward.

In a paper of 16th December 1980, new objectives were proposed. This paper is the first document I found which uses the term 'carers'. Essentially, the objectives proposed aimed to provide help for all those caring for elderly dependants. By June 1982 the Charity Commission had agreed to the new objectives and following the requisite legal procedures the Council was renamed, as from September 6th 1982, the National Council for Carers and their Elderly Dependants. Although the charity had given itself a new life, it is fascinating that a core group saw the original tasks as having been accomplished. There are few charities where that happens. Equally, as we shall see, it was good for carers as a whole that the Council was reborn and that its hard won expertise was not simply moth-balled. Yet even as the Council debated its new role, a highly significant development was occurring in, as they say, another part of the city, namely the founding by Judith Oliver of the Association of Carers, and it is that which now requires discussion.

V

The Association of Carers 1981-1988

During the early 1980s there was undoubtedly acrimony between the Council and the Association, some of which can be put down to personalities and some to a different philosophical approach to the issue of carers. Both organisations contributed to the increasing profile of carers, but the Association's much wider remit was a vital factor, though it also carried with it heavy organisational demands. To anticipate the history – the merger of the two charities in 1988 brought huge benefits to the carers' movement, combining as it did the very different strengths and skills of both bodies. The formative years of the Association now need to be considered.

Judith Oliver, the founder of the Association, was herself a carer, having a disabled husband as well as a young family. Juggling the two sets of family demands made her realise there was not, in fact, anything approaching care in the community. With a grant of £400 from the King's Fund she interviewed carers around the country to discover their experiences. The need for an organisation to support carers was evident. Media coverage generated hundreds of letters encouraging the formation of an organisation. The Association was formally established on September 1st 1981, aided by an unsolicited grant of £9879 from the Equal Opportunities Commission. There was further good fortune when a company in Preston, Vernon-Carus, offered to do all the printing for the Association and to provide PR and marketing advice.

The Association's aim was 'to assist and support anyone who is leading a restricted life because of the necessity to care for a person who is mentally or physically handicapped or ill or impaired by infirmity'. At an EGM in March 1984 the Association's aims were extended to include those who had had a caring role during the preceding two years. It was a self help organisation *of* carers, not *for* them. 'Carer' was self-defined, it was not for others to say who was a carer. Self-definition was viewed as empowering. The term 'carer' was, as we have seen, appearing in the Council's documentation by 1981, but it was not as aggressively promoted as by the Association. For example, in 1982, Judith Oliver urged carers to 'come out' and make their case heard.

The focus on carers was as important to the Association as had been the focus on single women to the Council, but the former was not well understood by the Charity Commission. The Association was initially refused registration as a charity, as carers were not a charitable object. The Association was asked to include 'dependants' in their name but refused to do so. It was not until September 1984 that charitable registration was agreed. The name and purpose had not been changed, but the constitutional aims now referred to the relief of poverty and sickness among persons who were in fact carers. Fortunately, the legalese in the constitution did not detract from the strong message embedded in the name of the organisation.

It is helpful in looking at the work of the Association to consider a number of themes, echoing those of the Council, namely campaigning, publicity, research, services and working with others. The first five years are critical and the momentum is at times almost overwhelming. 1986 was something of a watershed as Judith Oliver resigned in that year. The management committee in May 1986 had discussed the future direction of the organisation with one paper saying that we 'should finish the first five years and then start afresh'.

CAMPAIGNING

The campaign with which the Association will for ever be linked was that to have the ICA extended to married women. This issue was raised by the Association at its AGM in 1983 and publicised by Sandra Leventon, a founder member of the Association. This built on the work of the ICA Steering Group formed a year earlier and comprising 50 groups from disability and women's organisations. The plan was to take a test case to the European Court of Justice, arguing that the Government's failure to make the ICA available to married women was a breach of the EEC directive requiring equal treatment in social security systems. The directive came into force in December 1984. The married woman carer who became the test case was Jackie Drake, a member of the Association. The European Court found in favour of Jackie Drake and was due formally to announce its decision on June 24th 1986. On the evening of the 23rd the Government declared that it would extend the ICA to married women.

The Council had been opposed to this extension of the ICA possibly because of reports that Norman Fowler, Secretary of State at the DHSS, had said he would abolish the ICA altogether rather than extend it. Such opposition from the Council was not its most glorious moment and helps to explain the Association's management committee's reference in 1983 to the 'precarious relationship' with the Council. The pressure on the Government was probably irresistible and realpolitik came into play in June. There had been a debate on carers in the House of Commons on May 1st 1986, with an opposition amendment calling for inter alia the extension of the ICA. The amendment had been defeated, but by agreement words were added at the end of the debate which included a commitment by the

Government to carefully consider any judgement made by the European Court with regard to the ICA and to make a report to the House. It acted rather more quickly than that.

The ICA campaign brought carers cash and recognition. The recognition was more publicly reinforced with the Disabled Persons (Services, Consultation and Representation) Act 1986. This was a Private Member's Bill sponsored by Tom Clarke who had drawn number one in the ballot. The Act covered many aspects of disability but the Association persuaded him to include a clause relating to carers, although that term was not used in the Act and was not in fact to be part of the official language until 1990. The Act was a huge step forward for carers for it recognised for the first time the right of the carer's capacity to be assessed when considering the disabled person's needs. It was intended to make community care more of a reality. Specifically, the Act stated that where

> (a) 'a disabled person is living at home and receiving a substantial amount of care on a regular basis from another person (who is not a person employed to provide such care by any body in the exercise of its function under any enactment), and

> (b) it falls to a local authority to decide whether the disabled person's needs call for the provision by them of any services for him under any of the welfare enactments, the local authority shall, in deciding that question, have regard to the ability of that other person to continue to provide such care on a regular basis.'

It is astonishing now to think that until 1986 carers did not have their needs and capacities considered when services were determined for disabled persons. Suffering in silence was now at an end, although the realities of implementation meant that carers' burdens were by no means over, but there was now official recognition of their needs.

The two events described above were the most visible examples of the Association's campaigning work. There were others of great practical importance which are much more low key. For example, in 1987 the Association produced an advisory leaflet, *One Way to Get a Break*, after Sandra Leventon had won a test case to obtain money from the supplementary benefit scheme to pay for substitute care in order that the carer could go away on holiday.

But much else was undertaken, particularly by the Director, drawing all the time on the experiences of members who numbered 1500 by 1983. In 1984 the TUC was asked to raise with companies and local authorities the issue of compassionate leave for carers. At least eight local authorities responded positively. From 1983 onwards there were various consultations carried out by the DHSS concerning community care and the Association was represented on all the working parties, notably on the DHSS Social Work Service initiative on 'supporting the supporters'. Questions to put to candidates in the 1983 general election were agreed and circulated to members and branches. The pressure from bodies such as the Association and its involvement with the DHSS was one of the factors which led to the Department of Health initiative in 1985, *Helping the Community to Care*. This in turn led to the Informal Caring Support Unit at the King's Fund, later termed the Carers Unit and then Carers Impact.

PUBLICITY

If the Council and the Association had one thing incontrovertibly in common it was their ability to achieve publicity, allied to research.

The clippings agency was sending the Association about 100 clippings every two months, a far higher rate than anticipated. The media profile was strong from the outset, with *The Daily Telegraph* running an article seven weeks after the Association was founded. The

1984 AGM reported that in the year 1983-4 60 carers had covered 250 conferences, radio, press and TV items. It was always the aim to have a carer do the talking, something the movement as a whole has always seen as one of its great strengths, as well as being a godsend for the media. The newsletter (10 times a year) had a tear-off slip asking carers if they would be willing to talk to the media, and as Judith Oliver said 'and talk they did'.

In February 1984 the BBC *Afternoon Show* featured Brenda Goldsmith, who was caring for her 87-year-old bedridden mother and husband with a back problem. It produced a lot of publicity, but the carer's comments on the event are worth noting given three days filming was reduced to nine minutes! She said 'if it will do any good, if it will wake anyone up... that is the main thing'.

Committee members, too, played their part. The archives list the talks given by Sandra Leventon; on average two to three a month in a busy year. Few voluntary bodies would generate such commitment and even fewer would perhaps have board members so knowledgeable as to be so actively out and about on behalf of the charity!

RESEARCH

Judith Oliver had, like Mary Webster, done some small scale research prior to launching the Association, and the importance attached to reliable data remained. There were two distinct sides to the research: finding out the numbers of carers and describing their experiences.

In 1981 Judith Oliver had estimated that there were 1.25 million carers, a figure that no one was in a position to dispute, certainly not in government. Subsequent national estimates (6 million) suggest the Association was not exaggerating its case. In 1983 Anna Briggs, then Chair of the Association, carried out a door-to-door survey entitled *Who Cares?*, in two areas of North Tyneside. The two samples of 286 and 341 had 13.6% and 15.8% respectively classifying themselves as carers. The age of carers was now emerging. In the Briggs' study carers were over 50 and up to 85.

In 1984 Sharon Bonney in a report called *Who Cares in Southwark?* estimated there were 4674 carers in one area of Southwark. Again, the age of carers was striking with 18% being women aged between 71 and 80. In total, 38% cared for their spouse, 28% for children and 23% for parents. Interestingly, only 12% wanted to stop caring. Southwark was the first ever local authority to appoint a carers' support worker, a move which for the Association was a turning point in terms of official statutory recognition.

Whatever the numbers, there remained the challenge of getting services to the carers. In its funding application to the City Parochial Foundation in 1987 the Association cited a survey which 'showed that of 542 carers, 83 per cent received no help whatsoever from statutory services, voluntary organisations or neighbours. Indeed, many said that the nature of the tasks which they had to undertake was too personal and intimate to ask non-professionals to assist'.

With regard to personal experiences, Judith Oliver wrote an account of the lives of 22 carers. In 1986 the LSE published *The Caring Process: Mothers and Daughters at Home*, a study of 41 women who had cared for their mothers. With carers providing so much of the front line publicity and creating so much media interest the individual-based research was perhaps less essential than previously. But what all the research showed was the need for services.

SERVICES

The Association was much more driven to develop services than the Council, though this was partly because of its much wider constituency. By the 1983 AGM it was reporting receiving 500 letters a week, and staff travelling 10,000 miles a year to give advice and support, with local groups mushrooming from 70 in year one to 300 in 1985, 22 of which were in London. The staff included part-time welfare advisers. It became clear that carers were suffering from 'information poverty' and the production of a sign post guide became a priority. This was issued in 1984; called *Help at Hand*, it was sent free to all members (over 1500) and 5000 copies were sold. The aim was to rescue carers from isolation. The demands for advice and information increased dramatically with the publicity of the Jackie Drake ICA test case. At the 1985 AGM the Chair, Val Hollinghurst, said that carers were now on the map. In 1982 Judith Oliver had called for carers to 'come out'. They had done so in huge numbers... and they were not going back in.

In addition, the Association received a grant from Southwark to manage its carers' support worker and the activities she developed. There was in 1986 active participation in two Government initiatives: the informal carers' support unit set up by the King's Fund and the three demonstration consortia in Sandwell, Stockport and East Sussex to explore ways of helping carers. Even more thought provoking was the increasing concern for young carers (under 21) first noted at the 1983 AGM. This is a theme I will discuss in chapter VII; suffice to say for the Association it was another immense burden in terms of both service response and publicity.

Working the way it did was perhaps the only option in its opening years, but by 1986 Judith Oliver, who resigned at the end of that year, reported that 'direct work with carers is reducing as a proportion of overall activities' and that the Association was becoming a facilitator instead of an operator. The work was also increasingly financially complex. It was argued that the way forward was to have a regional structure. Funds were secured by 1987 for a London regional officer.

Very shortly after Judith Oliver's departure the staff reported to the management committee that they were overworked and 'dreading each phone call' in the office. Funding had become increasingly difficult, with the DHSS stimulating more work because of its initiatives but not providing more funding for the Association. In these circumstances it is hardly surprising that a merger with the Council, despite the previous frosty relationship, seemed a constructive way forward. Before looking at the merger I want to reflect on the Association's attitude to working with other bodies.

WORKING WITH OTHERS

Today it is virtually a sine qua non for directors and their organisations to excel at networking. As I have attempted to show, the Council always sought the support of a wide range of organisations in its campaigning work, however much it stood aside from the Association. The Association, too, was keen to have links with like-minded organisations. Its first annual report referred specifically to its liaison with other bodies. But where the Association was distinctive was in its wish to work in harness with those charities concerned with disabled persons. There has been, historically, a tension between the two movements, carers and disability, to which I shall return. Judith Oliver's argument was always that it was not a case of carer versus the cared for, but that both deserved better. It was an argument that was to be particularly strong in the case of young carers.

The 1983 AGM mentioned the work with such charities as the Alzheimer's Society and Contact a Family, both concerned with aspects of disability. A carers' consortium was formed in 1983 consisting of the Association, Contact a Family, Home Start Consultancy and Cope. Articles were written, for example in newsletters for organisations concerned with spinal injuries. The Association sought to be as inclusive as possible. It left its mark in many places, but as I have already suggested, by 1986 it was organisationally hanging on by a thread. I now want to discuss the paths in both charities that led to the merger between the Association and the Council.

VI

The merger in 1988

Early in 1987, approaches to the Association were made by the Council to consider closer working together with a view to 'organisational unity'. The Council's Branch Conference in March 1987 gave a warm reception to Val Hollinghurst, Chair of the Association, who spoke on the theme 'Partners not Rivals'. The Conference felt that both organisations should cooperate fully and that union was strength. The sixth AGM of the Association in October 1987 resolved that a merger between the two organisations 'is approved in principle and that the officers and management are instructed to proceed accordingly'. A parallel resolution was passed by the Council. Both sides agreed that the reasons for a merger were compelling, namely:

- their aims are very similar
- their constituencies overlap
- they are both seeking funding from the same sources
- there is confusion for the general public
- there is confusion for carers
- there is duplication of effort and consequent waste of resources
- locally and nationally there has already been satisfactory cooperation.

A steering committee (which I chaired) was set up and on May 14th 1988 a merger had been achieved and Carers National Association (CNA) was formed. The merger negotiations were, like all mergers, complex and overlain with a great deal of feeling on both sides. As a funder of both charities I was able to take a very practical line that funders would find it increasingly difficult to support two such similar bodies and we knew the DHSS held such a view. The meeting I most remember was when we debated at length whether carers should have an apostrophe 's' or not, thus indicating whose organisation it really was: an important and symbolic moment. Mergers between charities are more common today, but they are never easy, and the effects can take time to work themselves out. In the journal, Disability Now, there was a letter in 1989 which argued that the merger led to many casualties. However, rarely – and I have been involved in a number – have mergers not ultimately been justified. This one was to more than justify itself. Before looking at the expectations of the merger I want to return to the work of the Council in the years leading up to the merger as it was not just the Association, following Judith Oliver's resignation, that was facing difficult challenges.

As we have seen, the Council changed its name and broadened its scope in 1982. Yet within a year it commissioned a feasibility study on the organisation to be carried out by Michael Power and Pat Taylor of Bristol University. At the same time it was reporting that there was less interest in joining local branches because the ICA was now available thus reducing motivation. The era of tough campaigning was deemed to be over, although as the Association was showing there was a lot still to be done for carers as a whole.

The Power report, *Carers in Transition: a Relief and Respite role for the National Council for Carers and their Elderly Dependants*, was published in 1984. It now reads as a seminal document and psychologically may well have paved the way for the idea of a merger. The authors analysed the membership as at December 1983. There were 5,221 members, of whom 60% were former carers, almost all being single women living alone. This fact alone suggested the Council had run out of steam. The needs were to provide relief to current carers and social support to former carers, and the local branches were emphasising the latter. To provide relief for current carers was a 'complicated job' and beyond the resources of many branches. The report recommended that the Council should take a strong role nationally and this should be recognised by the DHSS. The liaison officer scheme should be expanded, with ten such officers being appointed over three years. Partnerships between services were needed to help carers. Immediate practical relief could be given to 2,000 member carers. £300,000 a year for three years was needed to develop the Council along these lines.

The immediate response to the report appears to have been muted, but by July 1985 the Council was determining its priorities as lobbying, liaising with other organisations, innovating policies and developing local branch networks. It had not fully absorbed the key message from the Power report about the nature of its membership. It also noted that the DHSS via the King's Fund was establishing in 1986 a carers' information and research body. This it viewed as duplication. It was an organisation somewhat under siege. At this point the Director, Heather McKenzie, announced she was leaving to go to Australia to look after her mother. A new Director, Jill Pitkeathley, was appointed. Jill attended her first Council meeting on December 3rd 1985 and indicated her style and vision by saying she wanted the letter paper to be redesigned and updated! Being known as Ms rather than Miss further indicated the new broom that had arrived. The club-like atmosphere in some of the branches needed to end.

It is just worth giving a flavour of the clash of styles that Jill Pitkeathley's approach was to engender. In an interview given in the late 1990s Dorothy Bennett, a founder member of the Council, said this as she looked back at her life and work as a carer: 'Of course this new head we've got, she reorganised us completely and now its called the Carers National Association. She was horrified that we used old envelopes. In the 1980s when the new Director came in, before you knew where you were the head office was blooming with umpteen typewriters, staff and that. Don't ask me where she got the money from. Now we never get asked to raise money for anything. I never add to my subscription when I send it each year. I think to myself, no, she can buy her own machines with somebody else's money.'

The Council's view of the King's Fund Unit as duplication (stay off my lawn) was a serious misreading of the climate at the time, especially as it had decided that its own top priority was lobbying. The Government's interest in carers and the establishment of the Unit was partly prompted by the campaigning work of the Association but was not a substitute for the voluntary bodies themselves. Given that Judith Oliver's estimate of 1.25 million carers was soon to be seen as a gross under-estimate, the Council and the Association were only going to scratch the surface without serious Government involvement. The Unit, coming as it did as the merger debate began, was important for two reasons. First, given the Government's interest in carers, it made it unlikely that it would continue to fund two national charities each concerned with carers. Second, the new merged organisation would begin in a relatively favourable political climate, for the Unit was to be significant in national service developments which was not the forte of either body.

The Social Services Inspectorate produced a paper on *The Role of Carers* in June 1990 which reviewed the Government's work to date. The Department of Health had since 1983 been involved in developmental work with carers through its Social Work Service (later the Social Services Inspectorate). It aimed to increase awareness of carers and their needs within social service agencies. There emerged a need to restructure services and their priorities, to respond more flexibly to carers, especially carers in minority ethnic groups 'who are often unknown to planners and service providers'. The Inspectorate was able to publish information about services and models of practice, such as *Fifty Styles of Caring* (1984), that would have been beyond the scope of a carer organisation. Its 1985 initiative, *Helping the Community to Care*, funded over three years three demonstration district projects to investigate the capacity of the voluntary sector in supporting carers. The evaluation showed the success of many of the voluntary schemes that were introduced. Part of the same initiative was setting up the Informal Caring Support Unit (later the Carers Unit) at the King's Fund.

The initial brief of the Unit was to improve the information available for carers. Consultative forums for carers were set up so that carers could have their voice heard and influence the work of the Unit. However, it soon became clear that carers were not getting services, not because they lacked information about them, but because the necessary services were not there in the first place. A 1990 research review report said 'so many carers have little or no experience of services to discuss'. So service development work became the focus. This was to be continued through an initiative called Carers Impact, funded by Government and a charitable trust. By now CNA was in existence and it became one of the lead bodies, along with health authorities, local authorities and other national voluntary organisations, in steering Carers Impact. Small multi-disciplinary teams worked in local areas to develop mainstream services for carers.

There was no dispute about the needs of carers. In 1989 the Unit published *Carers' Needs – a 10 Point Plan for Carers*. The challenge of providing the support and services to meet those needs remained. In fact, much later, in 1998, Carers Impact published *The Carers*

Compass: Directions for improving support to carers. This was aimed at the NHS and it found 'patchy and uncoordinated support' for carers. Carers' needs were not that easily met. This was to be also shown by the community care debate that began in 1986.

Even before the merger took place, the evident value of a powerful carers' voice became apparent with the Audit Commission Report, *Making a Reality of Community Care* (1986) and the subsequent Griffiths Report, *Community Care: Agenda for Action* (1988). This national activity and attention coming so soon after Jill Pitkeathley's appointment helped lay the foundations for her success as Director and gave the merged organisation a very strong platform on which to build. The movement's impetus stems from the Griffiths report allied to the Department of Health's initiatives outlined above. It is worth reflecting on the impact of the Griffiths report before examining in more detail the underlying reasons for the success of CNA.

Social policy produces spray-on words with regularity. In the 1970s 'community' had become such a word, carrying with it a feel-good element and being difficult to argue against. When attached to care it was clearly a vast improvement on anything institutional that had gone before. Conceptually, that was right, but what mattered more was how it worked out in practice – as it always should be. Previous reports on the mentally ill, the mentally handicapped, the physically handicapped and the elderly had all envisaged community services as the way forward. By the mid 1980s it was of concern to many that community care was not providing the answer. Was it really as cheap as first thought, and, if so, where were the savings coming from? Were there hidden costs? Did anyone now know what was happening in the community?

The 1986 Audit Commission report was highly critical of the then state of community care. An attractive policy had to become reality. The services were in disarray and certainly not value for money.

Carers barely figured in this report. The Government's response was to invite Sir Roy Griffiths to review the policy of Community Care. An advisory group was formed and Jill Pitkeathley was one of the group. Thereafter, carers were rarely off the agenda. The report itself stated that 'a failure to give proper levels of support to informal carers not only reduces their own quality of life and that of the relative or friend they care for, but is also potentially inefficient as it can lead to less personally appropriate care being offered. Positive action is therefore needed to encourage the delivery of more flexible support, which take account of how best to support and maintain the role of the informal carer'. Although the Government did not respond to the report until November 1989, the report in fact led to the NHS and Community Care Act 1990, which incorporated National Assistance Act provision.

As the NHS and Community Care Bill was going through Parliament, its importance was further underlined by the Fifth Report of the Social Services Committee 1990 which addressed the issue of caring and called for more practical and financial support. The fiscal arguments were picked up again by the Social Security Advisory Committee report in 1992. The political momentum behind the carers' movement was, if not unstoppable, certainly awesome.

Although the implementation of the NHS and Community Care Act was in fact to be delayed until 1993, everyone agrees that this was a key turning point for the carers' movement and, whilst not everything has been plain sailing ever since, that assessment stands. The new merged organisation could look back on the efforts of Mary Webster and Judith Oliver and all those, known and unknown, associated with them and know that a significant step had been taken.

The history of the next two decades is predominantly one of success, but before looking at that period in detail it is necessary to pay attention to three aspects which play a part in the overall history.

These are young carers, the disability lobby and the emergence of organisations with a carer focus but not necessarily defined as carer organisations. They raise practical as well as almost philosophical issues and weave in and out of a carers' history.

VII
Three key issues

YOUNG CARERS

The Association of Carers was first alerted in 1982 to the existence of young carers by a telephone call to the central office in Kent by a young mother with multiple sclerosis. Although she had a home help and other support from the local social services department, the only other person in the household for the majority of the day was her four-year-old son, as her husband had left the marriage being unable to cope with his wife's disability. She telephoned because her son had just had an accident in the house. Because the kitchen was not adapted to accommodate her wheelchair, he had to do things such as taking out of the oven the casserole which had been put there by the home help, who had left. He had done so without using oven gloves.

An enquiry by the Association and a subsequent awareness campaign revealed some truly astonishing stories of the part young carers played in their families. Governments are often resistant when new concerns are put to them. Their agendas are already too full, and Judith Oliver found the Government in 1984 was no exception. She experienced the Department of Health as 'hostile and unbelieving'. This was to change, but it is a small example of how the campaigning bodies have to be in it for the long term, longer often than ministers stay the course.

On 13th November 1984 a meeting to discuss the plight of child carers was held in the House of Commons, sponsored by Jack Ashley MP. Judith Oliver spoke, together with Nadia Bocock, the senior welfare information officer of the Multiple Sclerosis Society. On 20th November Tony Newton, Secretary of State for Social Security, met a deputation of young carers and he followed that up by announcing he would look into why children were having to look after disabled parents. There was extensive media coverage in both national and local press showing all too sadly just what a good story young carers were, which for the carers' movement was attractive for PR but also a warning about possibly being sidetracked from the main work. The obvious attraction to the media is best illustrated by the headline in the Daily Mirror of November 13th 1984 covering the story of a nine-year-old carer: 'Heartache of a little angel.'

One of the Association's case studies used in the public debate showed the dilemma. 'Susan is aged 12 years and her mother a MS sufferer abandoned by her husband. As a result, Susan now works a 17 hour day. It starts at 5.30 a.m. when she gets up to help her mother with toileting and dressing; she then does a full day at school before returning home to do the shopping and household tasks; her day ends at 10.30 pm when she puts her mother to bed. Susan was presented with an award by a national woman's magazine for her courage and dedication. We too applaud her, but worry about a society which allows such situations to exist.'

The Association had by 1984 estimated the number of young carers (defined as under 18) as 5,000 to 10,000 out of about 1.5 million carers in Britain. It said 'we are concerned about young carers in several respects. Firstly, is it appropriate for a young person to handle incontinence, menstruation or severe mental disturbance? Secondly, we meet many young carers whose education is greatly affected by the school time which they miss and the inability to concentrate at school. Lastly, we meet people in their 30s and 40s who have been carers from childhood to the death of their parents. They are usually confused, immature and unemployable. Is this really what 'care in the community' is about?' After a feature on Woman's Hour in January 1987 one man wrote in to say that he had been a carer for 25 years from the age of 14 and concluded that, though his mother's death was a relief, 'I am left with the damage that something which is longer than a life sentence has done to me'.

No one wanted to stop a local businessman presenting a new bike to an outstanding local young carer, but at the same time the wider social policy issues needed to be addressed. So, for example, the Royal College of Nursing at its AGM in November 1984 gave its full support to the Association to remove the need for there to be young carers. As the Chair said they 'are being deprived of their right to be children'. This was echoed in the title of a later (1992) Barnardo's report on young carers, *You Grow Up Fast As Well*.

The tension between the acknowledgement of the individual young carers and the broader social policy picture was well illustrated when in 1987 a public relations firm ran the Care Bear Caring Campaign to find a caring and unselfish child who thought of others. It was won by a young carer who among other things got her lifelong wish to be a bridesmaid. The *Today* newspaper ran a feature 'A Child shouldn't have to be a Hero' which was viewed by the firm as just cynical journalism. The Association sought to give the wider picture to the firm and tried unsuccessfully to enlist its help for the Association. Five years later, in June 1992, Jill Pitkeathley drew to the attention of the CNA management committee the importance of not participating in carer competitions, a policy which she and her staff had long upheld. Not least among the reasons was the tendency of such competitions to exploit certain groups of carers such as young carers.

Once the plight of young carers had been discovered, the momentum around it was virtually unstoppable. From 1984 to 1999 there were 166 articles and research reports on young carers and these are only the ones in the archives; I have come across many others. So, at least once a month for 15 years there was a significant media piece on young carers. Government recognition came with a Department of Health grant in 1989 for two years to fund a young carers post at CNA. The worker began in January 1990 and later reported that he had found 'no work going on to do with young carers and voluntary schemes in the country'. The scene was to change quite dramatically, for by the mid-nineties there was a sudden increase in young carers' projects, with job advertisements appearing at the rate of one a month.

Some today are very critical of the way the carers' movement 'exploited' this interest. Carers UK will not now do any media work on young carers. Three concerns dominate. The first is that by emphasising the 'little angel' or 'hero' role, the disabled person being cared for is too easily seen as a burden. Second, the argument for improved services for those with the disability gets lost. Third, failure to provide those necessary services leads to false trails. For example, it is not good practice to provide home tuition for young carers who have had to miss schooling; it is good practice to provide the services to ensure they do not miss schooling in the first place. The numbers remain high, with the 2001 Census showing there were 116,000 carers aged between 5 and 15 years old. There have been three national surveys of young carers from 1995 to 2004. Although these surveys show some improvement over time in the situation of young carers there is still a long way to go. For example, 22% still miss schooling and 20% of the families have no support services apart from the young person's involvement in a young carers project, of which there are now

200 compared with 36 in 1995. Hardly surprising then that Judith Oliver, now the chief executive of Disability Yorkshire, feels even more strongly than she did 20 years ago. For her, it is not an issue where time gives you an 'on the one hand and on the other' kind of perspective. The disability movement feels the same and it is to their relationship with the carers' movement that I now turn.

THE DISABILITY MOVEMENT

If the carers' movement has been marked by its success, then equally that is true for the disability movement. 'Carer' became a new term to describe an old situation. 'Disability' became the new term to replace words such as 'cripple' and 'mentally defective'. As an aside, it is worth noting, at a time when political correctness is under attack, that words do convey attitudes and prejudices and that there are very good reasons why we no longer talk, say, of cripples.

It is not appropriate here to write the history of the disability movement, but its development alongside that of the carers' movement has not been without its tensions. We noted in chapter IV that, from the beginning, the Council had included on its committee a representative of the Disability Income Group. This Group had its origins in March 1965 with a letter to the Guardian by two disabled women, Megan du Boisson and Berit Moore, asking for support for the recognition of the 'right of disabled persons irrespective of the reason for that disablement, to a pension from the State to enable them to live with a reasonable degree of independence and dignity in their own homes'. The organisation was to focus on the financial aspects of disability, hence its affinity with the Council. Generally, however, the Council was not drawn into strong arguments with the disability lobby, primarily because of its very single minded approach to its constituency and its emphasis on the fiscal issues. There was greater potential for misunderstanding or even conflict with the Association, because of its much wider brief.

At its core, the criticism by the disability movement is that carers 'prop up the system', even that they are 'oppressors' undermining the independence of the person with a disability, stereotyping them as a burden and making it less likely that proper statutory services will be provided. Young carers portrayed as heroes is the best evidence to support this analysis in the eyes of the disability lobby. It can be a fierce debate. Jill Pitkeathley was accused by some of putting back the cause of disability because of her highly successful work in promoting the cause of carers. The paper prepared for the Social Services Inspectorate in June 1990 noted 'it is also important to recognise that there is a body of opinion among disabled people that feels unhappy about the emergence of the carer in legislation and other policy developments. It is uneasy about the effects of an assessment process, for example, which may be 'biased' towards the needs of the carer since it is argued that professionals find it easier to identify with carers'.

Some of this conflict had already been played out in the passage of the Disabled Persons (Services, Consultation and Representation) Act 1986, where carers appeared in legislation for the first time. For instance, under the Act local authorities were required to have regard to a carer's ability to continue to provide care on a regular basis when assessing the needs of a disabled person. Carer groups wanted much stronger wording in the Act, but the disability lobby was concerned that more emphasis on the carers would only dilute the effect on disabled people, so the case was not pressed as hard as it might otherwise have been. Carers' needs remained acknowledged, but not at the expense of the primary beneficiaries of the Act, disabled people.

Such ideological conflicts are not uncommon in the voluntary sector and in fact are not usually resolved by one side 'winning'; the practicalities on the ground prevent that. The deaf world has had some strong debates around cochlear implants. The alcoholism world struggled with the argument around controlled drinking versus absolute abstention. I mention these examples (and there are many others) only to show that we should not become too perturbed by these kind of divisions. A uniform approach to some of society's most enduring challenges would hardly be plausible. Where do we go if, as studies frequently show, a proportion of disabled people want a family carer? The Association's report in 1987, for example, was entitled *Can a Carer say 'No'?* Many funders in fact finance charities on both sides of these arguments, as the certainty on either side is rarely totally convincing.

Judith Oliver, over 20 years ago, put it as well as anybody in trying to bridge the gap between the two sides: 'We were on the side of disabled people and acting in their interests too. Because from the start, we argued that disabled people deserved better than to be looked after by one (usually), exhausted (usually), possibly resentful person who was being used as a doormat by statutory authorities. We were saying that the system did neither side any good. It tied disabled people to one person who might not even be the person they would choose to have care for them.'

The carer/service user conflict is explored in some detail by Luke Clements in his book *Carers and Their Rights – the law relating to carers* (2005). Under the Community Care Directions 2004, a Circular gives general advice as to appropriate local authority responses where there is or may be conflict between a carer and the disabled person. Clements analyses the legal position where a disabled person refuses a community care assessment or where a disabled person refuses community care services. He refers to Section 2(3) of the Carers and Disabled Children Act 2000 which contains a provision designed to get around the problem of a disabled person who refuses services that would be of benefit to them and would also make a carer's role less onerous. The practical examples cited by Clements show only too clearly the careful work that has to be undertaken to resolve these conflicts. Reports from the Local Ombudsman suggest that councils have been too ready to take the disabled person's refusal at face value, when resolution would have been possible. Even though a disabled person may have behavioural difficulties leading to exclusion from services, the obligation is on the local authority to work with this problem and find a resolution. Carers are not just to be left high and dry, nor is their voice the only voice, but the resolution of some very testing practical problems indicates that for both carer and disabled person it is not an ideological dispute.

OTHER CARER ORGANISATIONS

Not to work together is rarely an option and in the 1980s there emerged two alliances that involved both carer and disability groups. These were the Caring Costs Campaign and the Carers Alliance.

The Caring Costs Campaign originated from a seminar in April 1987 which grew out of the former successful campaign to extend the ICA to married women. There were over 30 organisations involved in the campaign and the vast majority were disability charities. All were concerned that despite the success of the earlier campaign social security provision for carers was still very poor. The stated aim of Caring Costs was 'to achieve an adequate income for all those who are engaged in providing a substantial amount of care, at home, for a sick, elderly or disabled person. Such an income should not depend on the carer's age, sex or marital status or their relationship to the person being looked after. Rather it should be in recognition of the work involved in providing care and the financial and other costs which this work commonly entails, as well as compensating for earnings lost or foregone while caring. All of these too often go unrewarded – poor recompense for the dedication of very many carers'.

To achieve this goal, the campaign aimed to publicise the extent and causes of financial disadvantage among carers, ensure that information about current social security provision was widely known and, in the long term, to obtain an adequate and comprehensive system of financial support for all carers. The campaign took on special significance in 1990 when the Government began a major review of benefits for disabled people and their carers. It is clear that CNA made a major contribution to the Caring Costs Campaign.

The Carers Alliance had its origins partly in an initiative of Jill Pitkeathley, when in the late 1980s she wrote to all the parliamentary consultancies to see whether one of them would undertake pro bono work for the Carers National Association (CNA). One replied, GJW, which had been founded in 1980 by Andrew Gifford, Jenny Jeger and Wilf Weekes. Jenny Jeger began to meet with CNA, Contact a Family and the Alzheimer's Disease Society, and that group in turn met with officials at the Department of Health. Jenny Jeger continued to support and advise CNA until her death in 1997. But there had also been cooperation with a few organisations working together on the Forum of the King's Fund Informal Care Support Unit. It was decided to widen the group and 30 organisations, mostly service providers, joined what was now the Carers Alliance. Disability organisations were involved and it became clear that there were common interests and common problems. Different emphases there may have been, but they were all working to the same end.

The Alliance was quite formally constituted with terms of reference and rules, perhaps a lesson for some of the rather vaguer 'partnerships' which are much in vogue today. The stated aim of the

Alliance was 'to provide a means for voluntary organisations concerned with the needs of carers to work together for the development and promotion of policies and strategies to meet such needs'. The function of the Alliance was to raise public awareness of the needs of carers, to enable member organisations to consult about their policies, both together and with outside organisations, to encourage good practice, to provide opportunities for information exchange and sharing of experience and to formulate joint policies and work for their implementation.

The benefits of the Alliance were that key organisations met quarterly, compared notes on a range of issues and agreed a small number of joint actions such as leaflets and meetings at political party conferences. Above all, it gave CNA the power to say in its press releases and political deputations that it had the backing of 30 carer organisations. The Alliance was driven by CNA. Not all the bodies involved were primarily carer based, but through the Alliance carer issues moved up everyone's agenda. One Health Minister described the alliance members as 'blue chip charities'. But when the Princess Royal Trust for Carers, established in 1991, sought to join the Alliance and was greeted with some resistance, it viewed the Alliance as a 'cartel'. Some of the difficulty of this early relationship probably lay in the Trust having been founded by the Princess Royal and leading business men rather than arising out of the immediate personal experience that was the hallmark of other carer organisations.

The range of charities in such groupings as the Alliance shows that by the 1980s the carers' movement was more than the newly merged organisation formed from the Council and the Association. As I have indicated above, not all saw themselves as carer based organisations, though there were clearly interests in common. Some fitted equally well into the children's lobby, the disability movement or the parenting lobby. The overlap does, however, exist and it is worth just mentioning a few of the charities which emerged in the 1970s. They, of course, have their own histories and I can only give a snapshot here.

Contact a Family was registered as a charity in 1979, having originated with community work in Wandsworth and Ealing in 1974. Self help groups had been started to help families of children with disabilities and ease the problems of isolation they experienced. The initial driving force, and first Director, was Noreen Miller, who went on to direct the Alzheimer's Society. It is now the leading organisation representing parents of disabled children – in effect a UK-wide parent carers' organisation. It is an organisation that has always had strong links with the carers' movement. However, the parents of the children who move on from Contact a Family when their children reach 18 do not see joining a carer organisation as a natural progression, though they would certainly see themselves as having a caring role. At the same time, it has been important to have Carers Acts (1995 and 2000) which have put parent carers on equal terms with all other carers. Perhaps one can only say that there are several roles that all carers play, but what matters is that the legislation and the organisations are in place to provide the necessary services.

The Alzheimer's Society (formerly the Alzheimer's Disease Society) was established in 1979. It seeks to overcome the impact of dementia for people with Alzheimer's disease and other dementias and those who care for them. It provides practical support and advice, campaigns for change, funds and promotes research and works to improve understanding and awareness of dementia in society. It now has 265 branches and over 25,000 members. Years of campaigning brought the Mental Capacity Act 2005 (England and Wales) which will give people with dementia and their carers important new legal rights. It provided a statutory framework for people who are unable to make their own decisions and establishes a right for carers and relatives to be consulted on the treatment of the person they care for. As an organisation it has always worked closely with CNA. In 1993, for example, the two charities together, as part of the Caring Costs campaign, submitted evidence to the Social Security Select Committee on VAT on domestic fuel and a broader paper on the costs of caring. Local branches of carers for people with Alzheimer's did develop into independent charities, and I recall at the City Parochial Foundation in the 1990s supporting the Hammersmith and Fulham branch with substantial grants to help it develop its respite care service.

Crossroads Caring for Carers began in 1974 when it provided services to just 28 families. In 2004/5 it provided 34,000 carers with 4.5 million hours of respite care through its locally based schemes across the country. It has young carers projects as well as those concerned with parent carers and children with disabilities. Its most recent annual report, 2004/5, makes several references to its engagement with national carers' activities, for example to work with others on ways to develop innovative services to enable carers to remain economically active, return to work or develop new career skills. One can only note, yet again, that such objectives were at the heart of the Council founded by Mary Webster, albeit for a more limited group of carers.

Even the briefest of summaries of the three charities above shows the overlap and the synergy across the carers and disability movements. Overlap here does not mean duplication, as the focus is different and specialised. But what the various organisations have recognised over the years is the value of strength in numbers and the power of a united voice when pressing for key changes from government. No doubt there have been times when funders have had to choose between equally worthy projects from carer based charities, but to date that does not seem to have seriously impeded joint activities and alliances. In much of the joint activity CNA took or was willingly given the lead, but it would be the first to acknowledge the influence and contribution of all the other carer related charities. The river that is the carers' movement has had many tributaries and no single account can do justice to them all. But then it is not a competition. Indeed in August 1987 the Manchester branch of the Association called a meeting to establish a local branch of Crossroads.

VIII

The new merged organisation

Although I refer to a new organisation, and indeed in 1989 it made sure it celebrated its first birthday in style, it was of course the heir to older bodies. The publication by CNA in 1993 of *A Stronger Voice – The Achievements of the Carers' Movement 1963-1993* showed how astute it was at rightly making the most of that history. We have already noted in Chapter VI the compelling reasons for the merger. What now needs attention is the mood of the time in terms of the aspirations and style of the new body. It was not until 1990 that a strategy plan was put to the management committee, and a business plan somewhat later, but documents relating to the merger clearly show the way it was hoped the organisation would go.

The merger discussions had understandably spent much time on such issues as membership, voting rights, the constitution, management structures, branches and the decision making mechanisms. The reasons for the merger were accepted. The 'manifesto' for life after the merger was less debated, but a clear statement was made at the time about the way ahead, to which there seems to have been no dissent. As we examine the almost 20 years since the merger, it is valuable to look at the starting position.

The future was powerfully envisaged by the Director, Jill Pitkeathley:

> 'Every report written about carers stresses that their needs are
> not being met and that the numbers are very large (at the

minimum 1.3 million) and increasing rapidly. This rise in numbers will continue for the foreseeable future, in view of the increasing number of elderly people, the effect on the disabled of advances in medical science, and policies of caring in the community.

The market for a new organisation – carers who need help and/or might become members – is enormous. The potential of the new organisation to attract funding is also enormous, given that most people are likely either to be cared for or to become carers at some time in their lives.

Current joint membership is around 7,000 which indicates that we have not even begun to scratch the surface. It does not seem unreasonable to aim for a membership of *at least* (their emphasis) 100,000 in 10 years time. It is necessary therefore, when thinking of the new structure, to ensure that it will be able to cope with rapid growth and always to bear in mind the size, professionalism and national importance of the organisation we hope to become.'

There was confident expectation of rapid growth. However, it was not envisaged that the new organisation would normally become involved in direct service provision, except for specialised projects. The aims as set out in CNA's first annual report were:

- to encourage carers to recognise their own needs
- to develop appropriate support for carers
- to provide information and advice for carers
- to bring the needs of carers to the attention of Government and other policy makers.

Special attention was paid to policy making. The qualities required by the new body to be effective in this area were:

- credibility – it must be seen to reflect the needs of carers
- urgency – the need for respite and relief and other services is *now*

- sensitivity – to the needs both of carers active in the caring role and of former carers trying to rebuild their lives after bereavement
- consistency – those making the policy must be available and reliable in the time they commit
- stability – adequate continuity of membership of appropriate committees is necessary
- skill – gained by knowledge and experience.

This was a vision rooted in some practical realities, though perhaps ignoring in some aspects the lessons of the movement to date with regard to the challenge of recruiting and retaining new members or the headaches of raising funds. The tension between the campaigner and the service provider roles was also not far beneath the surface; even the specialised projects which were to be allowed came to present their own particular problems. Nonetheless, as a clarion call at the time of a sensitive merger it was invaluable. It is just that, on arrival, the promised land generally turns out to be rather different than envisaged, nor are the pathways trouble free.

Although there is little doubting the overall success of the carers' movement, it has not all been straightforward and it is instructive to look at three issues that have surfaced regularly, presenting problems for the organisation at the time. These are finances, membership and branches. Like all voluntary organisations, there have also been the usual conflicts within and without the charities. I have already referred to the tension between the Directors of the Council and of the Association. Committee members at various times did not always see eye to eye – one letter refers to 'explosions' at the committee meeting – but detailing this tells us little about the movement and is only par for the course. Personally, I always think of Cabinet meetings as a voluntary sector committee, and then political accounts and explanations of them become much clearer!

NOT ALL PLAIN SAILING

FINANCE

After the merger, the committee and staff might well have reflected on two very different financial events in the history since 1963. The first was in 1974, when the Joseph Rowntree Social Trust, which had given the Council a grant of £5,000 a year for five years, wrote to ask if, in view of the Council's healthy financial position, it would consider postponing claiming further instalments of the grant, as other charities were in greater need. The most the Council was prepared to do was to postpone an instalment of £2,500. Enterprising fund raising and legacies had largely contributed to this situation. Incidentally, legacies have continued to be an indispensable element of the income of CNA, which in September 2001 was renamed Carers UK better to reflect the fact that it is a membership organisation. The finances have perhaps never been as healthy as they were in 1974.

The second incident might be viewed as more familiar. In March 1984, the Association was down to its last £200, so Judith Oliver rang the Department of Health to ask for money, not least because all the work the Association was doing was at the Government's behest. Very soon, £4,000 was forthcoming and the charity survived. Anxiety about the funding was never far away from the mid-1980s onwards.

However, until 2003 there was not a major crisis. Raising funds was hard work and most years began with a deficit budget. What turned the deficit around was the funding networks of the Director, which of course grew over the years, the committee's confidence in the Director to balance the books, opportune legacies, Government initiatives sympathetic to carers, and the emergence of new funds such as Comic

Relief and the Big Lottery. The confidence in the Director was vital, as from time to time projects were undertaken for which all the funding had not been secured but which the Director argued were vital to do: funding would be found. It was a culture which worked.

With the arrival of a new Director in 2000 the culture was bound to change, if only because the funding skills and networks of an established director cannot be replicated in a new one. The style and tone will be different and committee members need to be more aware of the different systems of support and advice that a newly appointed director will need. No financial crisis has a single cause and the extremely serious financial problems which hit Carers UK in 2002-3 were no exception. By the time of the annual accounts of 2004-5, the charity was able to look back on 'two turbulent years' and report a healthy financial position. But it had been close. Coming near to collapse is not uncommon in voluntary bodies, and most come through it (I have personal experience of several). It is as if sometimes it has to happen, in order for an organisation to lick its wounds, learn lessons and discover new strengths.

BRANCHES

Branches have, from the outset, been a feature of the carers' movement, and are one of its strengths, but they are not without their own challenges. Without branches, the movement would probably not have succeeded and their formation was always encouraged. At the very least they provided support for carers locally and a source of hard-won experience-based information for the lobbying role of the organisation. Anecdotes may get you the interest of a politician for a moment, but winning campaigns requires evidence, and the branches provided that, either through their combined case histories or by providing the sample base for professional researchers.

Carers UK had 80 branches in 2006. In 1982 the Council had 46 branches. In 1986 the Association said 300 carers groups had been established, which may not be identical to branches but conveys the Association's momentum in the 1980s. The minutes and reports over the years, however, show clearly that the role of the branches was not always well defined and that their relationship with the national organisation was at times ambiguous, if not fraught.

The Power Report in 1984, to which reference has already been made, said that providing relief to carers was a complicated job and beyond the resources of many branches. Some branches by the time of the merger had become more like clubs of former carers rather than obvious havens of advice and support for new carers. Some wanted a strong say in the way the organisation was run, such as the branch which objected to the new logo in 1989 as it had not been consulted. Others felt they received insufficient financial help from the organisation. Staff felt that they were too thin on the ground to establish and support branches, most of which could not just be left to sink or swim; branch activity could reflect badly just as easily as favourably on the national body. If branches were needed, then they had to be nurtured. In 1990 the Director was aware of the 'financial and emotional' pressures on the branches. By 1993 it was clear that they should not employ staff, though in 2005 six branches were acting as employers!

In July 2004 the Board approved a grant to appoint a consultant to review the role of branches in Carers UK. The report in June 2005 was probably the most thorough the organisation had ever received. There was a great deal of difference as to how branches saw their role; failing membership was a concern; branches again differed as to how far they wished to be involved in the strategic work of the national body; the lobbying and campaigning role of Carers UK was highly valued; the relationship with Carers UK was not straightforward and communication between the branches and the national body needed to be improved. Elements of this analysis echo down the years, which is not to diminish its import. Rather, it is to say there is no neat answer to the national body – branch conundrum and perhaps never will be. Time and energy are required to make the relationship work and, as the minutes show, over 40 years these demands can be considerable.

MEMBERSHIP

For much of the history, concern about the numbers in membership was a regular item in many reports. There was never any worry about the enquiries for advice and information, as in fact these were invariably more than the office staff could cope with, but the individuals who rang or wrote in for advice did not take the next move and become members. The organisation might have had difficulty if they had. The Power report had shown how much work would be involved in raising the membership level to 10,000, let alone the 100,000 seen as the visionary target by Jill Pitkeathley five years later. It was further complicated in that not all members were in branches or indeed required to be. Members, like branches, gave credibility to the campaigns and the public statements, and rightly so, but with an acknowledged 6 million carers in 2006 no organisation could hope to do other than directly embrace a fraction of them. All carers benefited from the legislation directed to assist them so that, provided there was a credible membership base, efforts to increase that base by a thousand or so were not going greatly to strengthen the argument for a particular Bill.

Over the years the reasons for the membership not increasing significantly were the subject of much debate and indeed effort to correct the trend. Carers weeks were always seen as a great chance to increase membership, but as in 1996, for example, the response was invariably 'still disappointing'. By 2001 it was felt that to set numerical targets was unhelpful and more effort needed to be put into understanding and profiling the current membership. At the end of 2005 a membership development strategy has been implemented which is intended to halt the membership decline continuous since 1997. For the present, the numbers have stabilised at 8,000, and that is strong enough to give any campaigning platform credibility. It is not, of course, the only platform on which the organisation would base any case. Its work is frequently in harness with other carer bodies, all of whom bring their own users and members in aid of any particular issue. As the Trustees' annual report for 2003-4 states: 'We remain in contact with hundreds of thousands of carers each year, who keep us informed of their situation, their needs and the impact that new policy and legislation has on their lives. The knowledge we gain from this contact informs our priorities.'

Membership organisations have great strengths, but also can carry with them constitutional complexities. I have sat through the AGMs of several membership bodies where the explanation as to just who can vote for whom is quite taxing fully to comprehend. In 2001 Carers UK had an appendix to one of its sub committee reports setting out the then membership voting structure. There were corporate members who could not vote. Individual members who could vote were in two groups, A and B. The A group comprised inaugural members, carer members and former carers within three years of the caring role. The B group were former carers more than three years after the caring role had stopped and supporter members. Then, getting the balance between current and former carers is by no means easy. When membership was reviewed in 2001 the Northern Ireland Committee argued strongly that current carers have too much on their plate fully to participate in all the work of the national body. Former carers have, however, the time and the relevant experience. It has to be said that achieving 100,000 members might have taxed the electoral system at the AGM! In the end finding the 'hidden carers' (the theme of the first birthday launch in 1989) has in a way become more critical than drawing in the lost members.

In this next part of the book I discuss what I perceive as the underlying reasons for the success of the carers' movement. Simply to give a chronological account of its many and varied campaigns does not fully explain the success. The information on any one of these achievements is considerable and in some instances a complete account would require a detailed analysis of the benefits system relevant to the particular achievement in question. That is another type of social policy history that certainly needs to be written. However impressive any individual success, such as an Act of Parliament, none is the end of the story; they are only punctuation marks in the movement's history. Indeed, no sooner has something been achieved but the organisation is already on to the next battle.

In thinking about the history from 1963 to 2006 a number of themes have stood out. Some have already been touched on in the earlier chapters and where necessary will be referred to again but the main emphasis or evidence will be drawn from the last 15 to 20 years.

WHAT LIES BEHIND THE SUCCESS

NUMBERS

Most campaigning bodies require data to support their case as without it they would be over-reliant on anecdote or case histories. Carers' organisations have always been strong on numbers, have made good use of them and have been in the fortunate position that the numbers have continually increased in their favour. They are moreover the kind of figures for which extrapolations for the future are relatively easy to make so no politician can hope that the issue will somehow go away.

From the outset, the Council drew on the Census of 1966 to show that there were 310,000 single women living at home with their parents, though not all were necessarily carers. By 1974 a seminal publication by the Council, *The Wages of Caring*, stated that 304,000 single women were in a caring role. When the Association was launched in 1981 Judith Oliver estimated that there were 1.25 million carers, extrapolating from local studies. The Council in 1984 was talking about a 'crisis in caring for the elderly' saying that over the next 10 years there would be 2.5 million people in the UK between the ages of 75 and 84. Valuable data was soon to emerge as, thanks to the Association's lobbying, the 1985 General Household Survey included for the first time questions about carers. This showed that there were 6 million people in Britain with caring responsibilities, of whom 1.7 million were caring for someone in the same household. These were astonishing figures and, above all, incontrovertible. The force of the demographic arguments was powerfully expressed in the 2001 Carers UK report, *It could be you, the chances of becoming a carer*. No government was ever going to be able to ignore these figures, though how generously it responded to them was another matter.

The Census in 2001 included for the first time a question on the provision of unpaid care which confirmed the figure of 6 million carers but was also able to provide much more detailed and authoritative information about the composition of this group, 11% of the population. This stark statistic tells us about today, but since the 1980s the carers' world has talked about the demographic time bomb, as life expectancy increases and medical expertise enables young people with serious disabilities to live longer. Life expectancy will be in the 90s in ten years' time, having been 65 in 1950 and 80 in 2000. By 2025 those aged

75 and over will increase to 7 million from 4.5 million today, and those 85 and over from 1.1 million to 2 million. We all read accounts of carers themselves being in their 70s or 80s; living to 100 is no longer rare. The workers at Carers UK will in 2037 be talking of 9 million carers. The time bomb has actually gone off. This is not a scare-mongering campaign (not unknown in the voluntary sector!) but publicly accepted data. As Madeleine Bunting writes 'we've been far better at discovering how to cure people than how to care for them'.

The numbers alone tell only half the story. It is who the 6 million carers are and what they do that makes the case so powerful. To be counted as a carer in the Census only requires you to be caring for at least one hour a week and, valuable though that may well be in any individual case, it is not the tough end of caring. In fact, 1.25 million people provide over 50 hours of care a week and, of this group, 200,000 also hold down a full time job. Poor health is strongly associated with caring and the greater the number of hours provided, the more carers' health worsens. Young carers (aged 5-15) now number 116,000 and at the other end there are 1.3 million carers over pensionable age. The richness of the data from the 2001 Census is quite overwhelming and has been powerfully harnessed by Carers UK. I shall look at some of it in more detail later. But the number of carers is only part of the story, as numbers alone are not the basis of a successful campaign. The other side of the coin is the estimated value of caring or, more tellingly, the savings to the state. Being able to make a financial argument out of the hard data has been a second underlying cause for the movement's success.

THE VALUE OF CARE

On 28th February 2004 the Prime Minister, Tony Blair, speaking on BBC Radio Four's *Woman's Hour* said that carers save the country £57 billion a year but in terms of benefits get very little of that back in return. These figures were based on care costs in 2000. They were published in 2002 in a Carers UK research publication, *Without Us...? Calculating the value of carers' support*. The Institute of Actuaries was a principal contributor to the work. The previous figure of £37 billion, published in 1993, had been based on data from the 1985 General Household Survey and the 1991 Census. As with the numbers of carers, what is crucial is that the figure of £57 billion is not disputed, leaving space for lobbying on other care-related issues and not having to be drawn into financial and statistical arguments which are always time-consuming and rarely resolved.

In terms of the movement's success, the fascination is in seeing how the question of the value of caring to the state developed from some initial rudimentary figures into such a telling actuarial argument. The Council had in 1974 calculated that the cost of keeping an elderly person in a care home was £1,500 a year, or £5,000 a year in a geriatric ward. However, at the time it never seemed to make as much out of this publicly as might have been expected. It was then not until the Family Policy Studies Centre's publication, *The Forgotten Army*, in 1988, that a national calculation was produced. This estimated that the value of caring to the state was £3.7 to £5.3 billion, which even at that time 'dwarfed state provision'.

These accepted estimates of the value of caring, even if not always translated to the benefit equivalent, are a key way of focussing the attention of the policy makers and have been a strong weapon in the movement's armoury. But there is a third element which, as it were, cements the other two, numbers and value, and that is the cause itself.

CARERS ARE DESERVING

Imaginative schemes to assist offenders and ex-offenders abound, and they are invariably cheaper than any form of institutional care, but the economic argument is not compelling when faced with the public's view as to what should happen to offenders. The latter are not regarded as deserving, or they are certainly to come second compared with, say, the victims. Politicians will not talk about 'deserving' and 'undeserving' and often in private may wish to move ahead of public opinion. The reality is that some causes are easier to argue for than others; one only has to see the results of radio and television appeals to be aware of that. The political language shifts and we may move from basic values, the importance of the family, to 'rights' and 'responsibilities', but much is coded and the notion of 'deserving' is never far away. The good fortune of the carers' movement is that although the language has changed and some of the welfare state assumptions been reframed, carers have never been a group that could be sidelined or viewed as anything other than doing their fair share.

As a group, carers were ever ready to present their cause to the media and since 1963 all the organisations have had to hand carers willing and able to tell their story, be it to the press, radio or television. They are stories that are almost impossible to distort, and certainly in all the archives I have not come across a case of any carer crying 'foul' when the story appeared. But, as I noted with the disability lobby, the carer case can be made so powerfully that it accidentally demeans the person cared for. Though 'deserving', carers should not be presented as 'selfless angels' as not only can it reduce the services for the cared for, but also let professionals off the hook, in so far as they do not take full account of the carers' needs. There is a thin line between admiration for the carer and taking them for granted.

Whatever the pitfalls in having such a deserving cause, one huge advantage was the fact that politicians on all sides could not oppose it, and this was to be of immense value in sustaining the success of the movement.

POLITICAL SUPPORT

A neat illustration of how various Directors kept politicians on their toes and how sensitive the various Ministers were to the carer lobby was an exchange of correspondence in early 1991 between Jill Pitkeathley and Stephen Dorrell, Secretary of State for Health. Dorrell had made what seemed to Jill Pitkeathley some ambiguous comments about carers at a Policy into Practice conference in January 1991, so she wrote to him for clarification. The reply on 1st March 1991 said: 'I am pleased to take this opportunity to reassure you that I fully endorse the Government's commitment to make practical support for carers a high priority.' He went on to say that the Department would be publishing two booklets, *Carer Support in the Community* and *Getting it Right for Carers*.

The political support over the years is significant. Two Secretaries of State for Health, Sir Keith Joseph and Virginia Bottomley, were especially helpful, but both had become engaged with the movement long before they were in the Cabinet. Sir Keith Joseph was a founder member of the Council in 1965 and was a tireless worker on its behalf, particularly with fundraising. Virginia Bottomley was influential in securing grants for CNA in the early 1990s but in fact had become a member of the Council in March 1976, going on to the executive committee two months later. At that time she was not even an MP.

In March 1986 Norman Fowler, Secretary of State for Health, made a major speech to the Birmingham branch of the Council, apologising for not having been able to come in previous years! He even stayed for questions, including one relating to the pending European Court judgement on extending the ICA to married women, to which he said he was 'sympathetic'. For over ten years Tony Newton, Minister at the DHSS in the 1980s, was highly supportive of the carers' case. He was especially helpful when as Leader of the House in 1995 he worked with

Jill Pitkeathley on the Carers (Recognition and Services) Bill which a Labour MP, Malcolm Wicks, had drawn tenth in the Private Members' ballot. Newton arranged for all the stages of the Bill to be read in one morning, so that the Bill was enacted. Normally, to be tenth in the ballot is simply not high enough to succeed. The Social Services Inspectorate report already referred to talked of 'the concepts of carer support and policies for carers' having 'captured the imagination of many professionals and service providers'. It should have added the politicians too.

In 1972 Sir Keith Joseph, unusually, invited representatives from the Council to meet with his civil servants to discuss their concerns. Governments and Ministers have huge agendas, and to be heard requires patient lobbying. The work in this area has been critical in understanding the carers' success.

LOBBYING

The Carers (Recognition and Services) Bill became law in 1995 and the term 'carer' was now enshrined in law. There was now a right to an assessment of carers' needs and a right for assessment for parent carers and young carers. This Act was an impressive achievement, but, as the Director said, for the Association it represented six months of lobbying and eight years of work. Lobbying is a lot more than shouting from the roof tops (though some modern campaigners do that) and the style and persistence of the carers' lobbying merits attention.

The National Carers Strategy was announced by the Government in June 1998 and launched in March 1999, and represents a very good example of the lobbying skills of the carers' movement. The start of this was in 1995 when CNA had successfully invited Tony Blair and Cherie Booth, both lawyers, to launch *Carers and the Law* at the Law Society. The contact was reinforced when in 1996 Tony Blair made a public reference to his mother's experience of caring for her husband who had suffered a stroke. The Director wrote to him saying how interested they were to hear of his experiences of a carer. Throughout the general election campaign the nurturing of the contacts continued, with a lot of hard work involved. When the CarersLine was launched by Cherie Booth very shortly after the election in May 1997, it was not luck that CNA happened to secure her presence, but the result of sustained and skilful lobbying around the cause of carers.

In a lecture to a Carers Conference in Wellington, New Zealand, in March 2005, Jill Pitkeathley gave her account of the lobbying and thinking that led to the emergence of the National Carers Strategy, and it is worth quoting in full. The context is that by 1997 CNA had realised that there were limitations to the effectiveness of the 1995 Carers Act, in that there were no funds earmarked for its implementation.

> 'At this point we decided against going for another Carers Act by the private member's route straightaway. This was to do with the political climate of the time. Tony Blair's Government had been elected and we felt we had a good chance of getting it to embrace carers' issues rather more enthusiastically than had been the case with the previous Government. The new Government was certainly wanting to appear a lot more caring than the previous one, they were promoting the idea of social inclusion as a political philosophy and carers were an obvious target group. Moreover, I had, to my great surprise been offered a peerage by the incoming Government, so that as a member of the House of Lords and now revealed as a Labour Party supporter I was able to have more access to ministers to promote our ideas.
>
> We decided to try to get the Prime Minister himself to launch a new strategy for carers so that it would command the highest possible support and backing. The tone we adopted at this time was of the greatest importance. We wanted to acknowledge the

progress which had been made thus far and build on it, not take the line that the previous Government was uncaring and this one was going to change everything. This is not always an easy position to communicate to politicians as you will appreciate, but a carers' strategy is only going to be as good as those who implement it. You need to keep your line as politically neutral as possible otherwise you risk alienating those who can make or break any strategy. Besides in politics one must always bear in mind that today's government is tomorrow's opposition and vice versa. Be politically aware and stay politically neutral however great the temptations or seductions offered by opposing parties. But do not be politically naive. Read the political runes and react to them.

The Government agreed to take our advice on this and Tony Blair announced the National Strategy in June 1998. Its terms of reference were:

- To assess whether any key needs of carers had been overlooked
- To clarify the Government's objectives for carers
- To set out an integrated strategy for future action
- To report to the Prime Minister in six months.

About this time I left Carers UK in order to take up a part-time position which better fitted with my new responsibilities in parliament. After a period of consultation, the strategy was launched by Tony Blair in March 1999. It included recommendations on four main topic areas:

- Employment
- Information
- Support
- Care for carers.

It also made reference to the changes set in train in the social security system which would benefit carers such as state second pensions. It drew attention to the particular problems faced by specific groups of carers such as young carers and carers from black and minority ethnic communities.

The announcement of this strategy in such a high profile way – carers were invited to Downing Street for the launch and it received massive media coverage – was of course of the utmost importance from a campaigning point of view as were two specific promises made in the strategy. First there was to be a specific allocation of money to local authorities to provide respite care for carers and a future power was to be given to local authorities to provide services directly to carers. This was the green light to the second piece of legislation which my colleagues in the carers' movement had been seeking – the right of carers to have not just an assessment of the needs but services suited to them as a result of that assessment. It was also a vindication of the decision taken at the time of the first Carers Act to take a small step and use it to build support for the next legislative step.'

During the above process CNA was far from idle! Four working groups had been set up in June 1998 to develop the strategy and CNA was represented on two of them, namely health and employment. When the strategy was announced CNA responded in two days, almost as a means of mutual reinforcement. All this was at a time when it had an Acting Chief Executive, Francine Bates.

It clearly would have been possible, with a new Government and the links CNA had with the Prime Minister, to have pressed immediately for another Act of Parliament. The longer term view was taken, as a national strategy ought itself to provide the basis for necessary legislation. This turned out to be the case when Tom Pendry (now Lord Pendry) secured a place in the Private Members' ballot at the end of 1999. With Government backing a new Bill, the Carers and Disabled Children Bill, was published on January 28th 2000 with its second reading due on February 4th. When passed the Act introduced new rights for carers and included the right to support services and for these services to be made available through direct payments and vouchers, such as vouchers for breaks. Two aspects to the passage of this Bill should be mentioned.

First, parent carers were not originally included in the Bill. For Contact a Family this was a devastating omission. Sustained and collaborative work between them and CNA led to the Act covering parent carers. Second, although the Bill had Government backing there was an enormous amount of work that CNA in fact had to do to ensure that the Bill met their concerns, not only on the inclusion of parent carers. A press launch was organised with a carer recounting her experiences, a fact sheet on the Bill was prepared and demand for information was high. Amendments were drafted, information put on websites and carers and carer organisations encouraged to contact their MPs with their views and comments. One can only reflect on the level of CNA lobbying input required even when there was a fair wind from Government.

The time and effort required for effective lobbying probably goes without saying, but there are other particular lobbying skills that the organisation demonstrated over the years that are worth mentioning.

First, whilst it is manifestly important to press forward on a specific issue it is also essential to sustain the momentum by picking up on any relevant matter. The correspondence with Dorrell cited above is a good example of that and there are many others. Keeping the authorities up to the mark helps maintain a climate in which it is more difficult for politicians to thwart the cause.

Second, the compelling case that carers undoubtedly have, and the case histories which drive it home, might so easily push the organisation into asking for jam today, rather than bread today and jam tomorrow. Even if the former is richly deserved, politicians are not noted for responding to pressure by saying 'yes, certainly you can have that and I am sorry for any delay'. In other words, realism and compromise have to be watchwords however hard at times that may be and especially if it is not always acceptable to the organisation or movement as a whole.

In February 1996 the Director stated that policy development should be 'achievable, sustainable and credible'. This was restated in 2004 when it was agreed that the Carers UK policy position had to be 'well researched including seeking out the real financial cost and grounded in the following principles – realistic, desirable and achievable'. So in 1989, for example, the Director urged realism about the community charge and its impact on carers, saying 'we must be aware of what realistically can be achieved. We cannot hope for a great reform of the legislation, but must work on getting minor amendments which will benefit carers'. A resolution put to the 2000 AGM to greatly increase the ICA was deflected by the argument that the level of the ICA should be that of the Basic State Pension and long term Incapacity Benefit. To have it likened to a 'wage' was to run the risk of carers being treated as 'employed'. There were other resolutions at the AGM which 'deplored' or 'condemned' Government action or inaction. Here the committee took the view that 'regret' was the more appropriate term and tone.

This grounded approach to campaigning was strongly expressed in the strategic plan for 2005-8 (which I shall discuss later). In the plan specific campaigns are identified and the criteria on which these campaigns will be based are set down as:

- to be in the interests of carers and former carers
- to be achievable
- to be well researched
- to have pragmatic solutions
- to draw on good policy and practice from across the UK, Europe and beyond.

At a strategic level, the Acts of Parliament invariably present a challenge as to just what to aim for and the 1995 Carers (Recognition and Services) Act is a good example. The Government wished to support the Bill (a Private Member's Bill introduced by an Opposition MP) but would only agree to carers having the right to their own assessment, not to services thereafter. Some saw agreeing to that as a 'sell out' but time has rather shown that just getting the Act was a vital first step. But also by accepting the Government's position on the big issue, CNA had scope to press on other issues such as securing the inclusion of young carers in the provisions of the Bill and bringing forward the date of implementation by a year to April 1996. When there are concerns at developments, the carers' correspondence with Ministers expresses disappointment rather than anger and always hopes that what is being proposed is simply the first step. No Minister has ever written back to say 'no, it is the only step'! Equally, however angry one is, conveying it to Ministers does not lead them to break down and confess to their failings.

The third skill in the carers' lobbying has been the capacity to see the Acts of Parliament as first steps and to sustain a follow-up campaign around the implementation. The Acts are punctuation marks in the history of the carers' movement, not the end of the road. Dr Hywel Francis MP, the sponsor of the Carers (Equal Opportunities) Act 2004, wrote after its successful passage: 'our next challenge is to support its effective implementation by local authorities.' Part of the movement's success has been the time and energy given to following up the legislation to see whether it has been translated into improved services for carers.

A very good illustration of why no achievement should be treated as a full stop is the Special Grant for carers paid to local authorities under the National Carer Strategy. For 2005-6 the sum was £185 million. The grant was aimed to enhance services for carers by allowing them to take a break from caring. However, from April 2004 the grant is no longer ring fenced. It is now a 'targeted grant', a phrase that suggests Carers UK and others in future will need to be extra vigilant. Councils will be inspected 'to ensure that carers are still being cared for'. Arguments about resources once again do not seem far off.

FOLLOW-UP LOBBYING

The NHS and Community Care Act 1990 had placed a duty on local authorities to consult 'private carers' in determining the services for the cared for person, which was a major triumph for the carers' movement. Implementation had been delayed until 1993, much to the formally declared 'tremendous disappointment' of CNA, but the delay was in part due to the need for the Department of Health to produce its implementation guidance. CNA was active in ensuring that the principle of the carer being consulted in determining services for the cared for was embedded in the guidance. It was also working closely with Age Concern, the Spastics Society (now Scope) and Radar over issues affecting older people and disability. There were worries about the Department of Health's guidance where it advised local authorities to reduce the risk that they were not meeting their statutory obligations by not recording, for example, unmet needs. In July 1993 Jill Pitkeathley reported to the CNA committee that legal advice had been obtained on challenging the Act and the subsequent guidance. Seven other major national charities were joining with CNA in this challenge. Test cases were being considered. Ultimately in March 1997 the House of Lords ruled in the Gloucestershire case that a local authority can draw up eligibility criteria which balance the need for help with the resources available.

The Carers Act 1995 was implemented in April 1996 and one year later CNA published two major reports examining the progress made in service delivery to carers. These were *Still Battling? The Carers Act one year on* and *In On the Act? Social services' experiences of the first year of the Carers Act*. The conclusions were not encouraging. The first study surveyed 1,655 carers. There were clear gaps between policy and practice at the local level: for example, 82% of carers had not asked for an assessment and where they had, only half had received the written results, though it was local authority policy to provide them. As the report concluded 'there is still some way to go before practice catches up with it [policy]'. The second report showed that although the Act had increased services for carers and awareness of their needs in local authorities there was a lack of resources available, which meant that carers had to compete with many other groups.

Six years later, in 2003, CNA published *Missed Opportunities: The impact of new rights for carers*. This study was a postal survey of 10,000 carers, of whom 1,695 responded, and of 10 local authorities. The conclusions again showed that there was still a lot to do for carers. 'Carers are often outside the social care system.' 'Chronic underfunding of social care is leaving carers to plug the gap with significant consequences for carers – poor health, no job prospects, strained relationships, even a disregard of their fundamental human right to family life.' In essence 'hard won rights have yet to deliver real choices for carers'. Some of these consequences are now being picked up in the current Carers UK strategies. In addition to following up the impact of the legislation, CNA has always been a constant campaigner around the overall situation of carers. We have seen from the very beginning how the Council used its research findings and kept its concerns on the agenda through such events as the National Dependants Week (now Carers Week), first held in 1969. That stream of activity has continued and has been instrumental in the overall success.

RESEARCH AND CAMPAIGNING

Lobbying and campaigning are, of course, interlinked. Here I am treating lobbying as work focussing on a specific outcome, such as an Act of Parliament, and campaigning as having a broader base. The latter is really to lead the debate on issues affecting carers, to work to inform and influence policy makers and to run public awareness campaigns. It is keeping the issue on the agenda of those who can bring about change. As we have already noted, credibility is a key value of this type of work so the campaigning has gone hand in hand with research. In effect it has ensured that carers have not, as an issue, slipped off the radar screen. I will give a few examples of how sustained and important this work has been.

In 1992 the *Listen to Carers* campaign was launched with the Speak up, Speak out theme. Issue Communications ran the campaign for nine months and it was monitored fortnightly. The three objectives were:

- to give 6 million carers a sense of permission to speak about their needs
- to instruct professionals in primary health care and social services to listen to the needs of carers and seek to meet these within available resources
- to stress to the general public (and indirectly the policy makers) the value of carers as providers of 95% of care in the community.

Although the Association viewed the campaign in 1992 as successful, research showed that many carers were not asking for an assessment of the person they cared for, so the campaign in 1993 was entitled *Ask for Assessment*. The key campaign objective was to encourage carers to ask for assessment, support and services and to persuade professionals to listen and take action. It should be noted that the combined budget for these two campaigns was £85,000.

There was not a campaign every year, but annual carers weeks continued, which were in essence a campaign without necessarily an identified theme. But even the basic (if one can so limit it) carers week was costly (£100,000 in 1999 for instance) and involved a vast amount of work (47,000 booklets distributed in 1999). The combination of the week with the publication of new research was always a strong statement. In 2000 the start of the carers week was marked by the publication of *Caring on the Breadline*. This was a survey of 2,093 carers which showed the poverty they were experiencing, especially those providing substantial amounts of care: cutting back on food, struggling to pay the rent or mortgage, forgoing holidays and so on. The call of the campaign was to 'hope the Government will work closely with us to find creative ideas to tackle carers' financial problems to counter the true costs of caring'.

The *Fair Deal for Carers* campaign in 2000 aimed to change policy to ensure that carers did not struggle financially because of their caring responsibilities. The four aims were:

- to raise awareness of carers' financial issues
- to help carers to identify themselves and seek advice about benefits etc
- to enable carers to speak up for themselves
- to seek policy changes which will increase the level of carers' incomes.

The title repeated that of the 1994 campaign, but that had been about getting services rather than financial resources. What is interesting about 2000 is that in January 2002 the Board was exploring possible future policy issues because of 'the success of the Fair Deal campaign'. Certainly there had been five improvements in the financial position of carers including access to ICA for carers over 65, extending ICA for 8 weeks after the death of the person cared for and an increase in

Carer Premium for carers on means-tested benefit. But by no means all had been achieved and, as a North of England campaign in 2001 and a national campaign in 2005 showed, there was much to do for carers beyond their financial situation, important though that was. One result of the campaign was the creation of an annual Carers Rights Day, the first of which was held in 2000. These are days in which to provide up to date practical information about carers' rights and to highlight the services provided by Carers UK. On Carers Rights Day 2005, 370 groups ran local events, a new booklet on older carers' rights was published, the *Carers Rights Guide* was updated and posters and other promotional material were launched. In addition, a new survey on older carers was underway for launching on the day.

In October 2001 Carers UK published *Health's Forgotten Partners*, which looked at how hospital trusts in the north west of England involved and supported carers through hospital discharge of the person cared for. Policy and practice needed to improve. Then in 2005 Carers UK published *Back Me Up* which detailed the experiences of 1,207 carers when having to deal with an emergency or unplanned event. Incidentally this was exactly the position facing Judith Oliver in 1980 which led her to found the Association of Carers. Organised back up for carers was still not in place and contingency planning was not part of the carer's assessment. Some good schemes were operating but they were few and far between. Judith Oliver would, it appears, not be much better off today than she was 25 years ago. At least with *Back Me Up* in 2005 there was solid research, telling case studies, a professional publication, a strong campaign and sound practical recommendations. Further research was then undertaken to look at good practice and this report is now in the pipeline.

One goldmine of new information to be quarried as a basis for research and campaigning is the 2001 Census which included for the first time detailed questions on unpaid care. As we shall see below, critical information is now available on the combining work and care. Other key issues are also being highlighted. For example in December 2006 Carers UK published *In the Know*, the second part of which examined carer turnover. Research into the latter combined data from the Cenus with work done by Michael Hirst in 1999 using the British Household Panel Survey. What Carers UK could now show was that every year there are just over 2 million people who start caring for the first time, which is over a third of the total number of carers at any one time, namely 6 million. But there is also almost the same proportion who cease caring each year. The report is also able from the Census to give carer turnover details for every local authority. What this then requires is for the authorities to ensure that information for those leaving the role who may, for example, wish to look at career opportunities or need more advice and support than is sometimes understood when one leaves a demanding caring role after many years.

One new aspect of the campaigning which would be totally unfamiliar to many previous workers in the carers' movement is the attention now being given to carers and human rights. In May 2006, Carers UK published a report, *Whose rights are they anyway? Carers and the Human Rights Act*. The report argued that the Human Rights Act could well be of value to carers. The evidence shows that carers' rights are being breached in three respects: carers' rights to life are not adequately considered; carers' rights to privacy and family life; carers' rights to be free from inhuman or degrading treatment. It will be fascinating to see how this campaign develops. It is broadening the agenda and showing all the imagination that has so often been demonstrated in the carers' history.

STRATEGIC DEVELOPMENT

The organisation's strategic plans have inevitably developed over time and have underpinned its work. It is instructive to see how they have broadened out. They have encompassed the issues of the day so that the Carers (Equal Opportunities) Act 2004, sponsored by Dr Hywel Francis MP and driven by Carers UK, is described by community care lawyer Luke Clements as marking 'a major cultural shift in the way carers are viewed'.

When, in early 1990, Jill Pitkeathley introduced her first major strategy plan, it met with a mixed response from the committee, some regarding it as 'splendid' whilst others said it 'lacked vision' and was insufficiently carer focussed. The fourth version was accepted and the Director saw the central task as 'transforming the CNA into an effective national voluntary organisation' with the 'working capital being the resilience, tolerance and stamina of staff and members'. By 1993 vision was more to the fore – 'to enable carers to speak with a stronger voice'. The three key objectives were stated as to provide information and advice for carers, to develop and maintain appropriate support for carers at local and national level and to bring the needs of carers to the attention of government, other policy makers and the general public. In March 1998 Jill Pitkeathley advised the committee that CNA should be positioning itself for the next century and that access to services should be the key external aim.

In the event the strategy plans for 2000-3 and 2005-8 were to represent quite significant changes without losing sight of the core needs of carers. The first was developed by Diana Whitworth, the Chief Executive from 1999 to 2003 and the second by the current Chief Executive, Imelda Redmond. For 2000-3, for example, there was a strong emphasis on working to ensure that the policies and practices which affected carers should deliver real choices, a decent and sustainable income and a quality of life which is acceptable to carers and those they care for.

The current operational strategy is the most expansive, as indeed today are most charities' modern day strategies. The vision is more all encompassing: 'We have a society where there is true equality for carers, where their role and contribution to their families and society is recognised, where they are fully empowered and where they are respected as equal and expert partners in the planning and delivery of care.' The six mission statements include securing full implementation of the legislative and policy rights that have already been achieved, promoting changes where needs are still not being met and having good information strategies so that carers have quality information about their rights. The five objectives of the plan covered campaigns for a fair deal for carers, policy improvements for carers, carer involvement, governance and management and work in collaboration and communication. All of these five were spelt out in great practical detail. Most importantly these were reinforced by a paper in September 2005 which set out the key performance indicators so that everyone would know just how far the strategic aims were being achieved. From time to time in the minutes over the years a lone voice had questioned the effectiveness of campaigns, one even saying they were 'mediocre'. Now it should be possible to answer such questions.

The detailed information about the planned campaigns given in the 2005-8 operational plan shows how much more holistic the movement had become. It is almost as if the early work, vital though it was, had dealt primarily with the tip of the iceberg. As more research was done and as carers spoke out ever more forcefully the needs and aspirations of carers required more analysis and attention. Much of this was reinforced by data now available from the 2001 Census. It is perhaps the nature of the caring role that issues are masked for a long time –

you cannot just walk away from it and you may not have the time and energy to raise your voice. One recalls the single women 'under house arrest' in the 1960s, a situation that had gone on far too long even then. It is also a question of the organisation having the experience, confidence and stability to focus on a wide range of needs. Getting to grips with these layers of need has been an essential factor in the movement's development. Before describing what I have called the coalescing of needs, it is essential to reflect that Carers UK has also ensured that it does not lose sight of carers' basic concerns. The foundations are, as it were, always being underpinned and that too has contributed to its success.

STRENGTHENING THE BASIS

At the AGM in November 2006 Carers UK announced that it was launching an investigation into the financial implications of caring which would involve revisting work last done in 2000. Evidence is now being gathered. The organisation has always been alert to the need to refresh its research data. Effective campaigning requires it. Proof of the importance of paying attention to the fundamentals is well illustrated by the report published in December 2006, *In the Know – The importance of information for carers.*

Carers have always regarded information as a key priority, as without it they cannot hope to understand and make best use of the 'system' of which they become a part when caring commences. The research studied 265 carers who had called the carers helpline on Carers Rights Day on 5th December 2005. The familiar issue of 'hidden carers' again emerged, as 32% had been caring for five years before they recognized they were a 'carer' and hence entitled to help and support. Over half of the total sample had missed out on benefits and support for over three years. This reinforces in detail earlier work by Carers UK which argued that £740 million a year in carers' benefits was unclaimed.

COALESCING OF NEEDS

The campaigns now seen as at the heart of Carers UK were listed in the strategy plan and elaborated in the Carers' *Agenda for Change* in 2005:

- better recognition for carers
- freedom from poverty and financial worry for carers
- respect for carers' own health and well being
- real opportunities to work
- full inclusion in all aspects of society.

This combination, even modernisation, was a powerful message as to what carers truly needed. There were, however, fresh slants and more coherence now being given to some older concerns.

Work, for example, had always been an issue since the 1960s, but was seen rather as a right to return to work after the caring had finished, or to be retrained as skills had been lost during the years of caring. Gradually, the whole work issue broadened out. In 1974 the Council commissioned research on working women with dependents. The Association made links with the TUC which called in 1984 for positive action in regard to women carers. The dilemma of combining work and caring responsibilities then never really went away. During the 1990s there were 50 or more articles, reports, conferences and books all discussing the worker carer problems. In 1993 a Junior Health Minister urged employers of carers to be more sympathetic to them. Voluntary organisations proposed codes of practice. At least two companies sought to reduce the anxiety of employee carers by setting up a 'granny creche' for carers' elderly relatives. In 2005, Carers UK knew that 80% of carers were of working age and 3 million carers already combined work and care. During the last two decades the challenge of caring and working had been kept on the agenda but good practice was not spread across the UK. Hence in the *Agenda for Change* Carers UK stated that 'many carers are still let down by inflexible service provision and restrictive benefit regulations'.

Early in 2006, ACE National and Sheffield Hallam University published a report for Carers UK, *Who Cares Wins: The Social and Business Benefits of Supporting Working Carers*. The arguments were now moving from the need for carers to have work opportunities to providing evidence that having flexible working arrangements that enabled carers to work and care had strong business benefits from both the managerial and employee perspectives. The research was an in-depth study of three very different organisations including a large Government department. An organisational commitment to diversity and inclusion is not just fine words but for these three organisations had tangible benefits for everyone. Carers want to work and care.

Health of carers had also been an issue from the 1960s with reference to exhaustion and depression in particular. Now there was information about the level of mental health problems among carers and there were 316,000 carers who described themselves as 'permanently sick or disabled'. The 2001 Census had shown that carers who provide high levels of care for sick or disabled relatives and friends are more than twice as likely to suffer from poor health compared to people without caring responsibilities. This issue was expanded on in 2004 with Carers UK's publication, *In Poor Health: the impact of caring on health*. The concept of social inclusion (and its potent opposite, exclusion) became a strong motif of the Labour Government in 1997 and has remained so. For Carers UK it is a powerful concept as it enables the organisation to bring together concerns that have always been there but are not so easily harnessed:

carers not being able to take holidays, having to give up work to care, reduced leisure opportunities and, for young carers, missed schooling.

In the fifth decade of the carers' movement no campaign seems more fresh and relevant than that which focuses on work, education and leisure. It encompasses the cultural shift already mentioned. This is not, of course, to underplay the campaigns around recognition, poverty and health which might be viewed as the bedrock, as without good health, for example, work and leisure are less achievable. The new dimension in the *Agenda for Change* merits attention.

The campaign is very characteristic of the movement for five reasons. It draws on carers' experiences. It relates to and builds on national research. It capitalised on the opportunity to promote a parliamentary Bill when Dr Hywel Francis MP was successful in the Private Members' Ballot and in December 2003 asked Carers UK to help him take a Bill through for carers on employment and lifelong learning, which resulted in the Carers (Equal Opportunities) Act 2004. It played into the Government's social inclusion agenda. Finally, it was able to translate the detail of the above into a practical and comprehensible campaign.

The issue of carers and employment had been given new life when in April 2000 the Government formally launched the Carers and Employment project, with four Ministers attending. This led to the Department of Health undertaking some small scale research into how far statutory carers' assessments considered the needs of working carers or those who wished to return to work. The DfEE was looking at work-life balance and agreed to consider carer-returners in that context. The training needs of young carers were also to be considered. However, all this development was given a major boost when in 2002 the Carers UK-led Action for Carers and Employment (ACE National) project was given three year funding by the European Social Fund's EQUAL Community Initiative Programme.

This project sought to redress the barriers faced by carers and former carers in entering, re-entering, or remaining in the labour market, through establishing a national partnership to influence the development of services and policy at local and national level. ACE National was evaluated by the Social Inclusion Unit at Sheffield Hallam University whose final evaluation report was published in July 2005. What is striking, as so often with carers' projects, is how it combined practical benefits for the 450 participating carers with a continuing impact on the policy agenda. Local projects were successful in offering individual support and training, especially with personal development and IT. On the broader front two successes illustrate the impact made. First, the ACE project developed with City and Guilds an e-learning pre-vocational training system and accreditation framework, especially designed for carers. Second, ACE established an effective Employers for Carers group at national level, whereas it had been more difficult at a local level. The Carers Act 2004 gave an extra opportunity to raise awareness of carers and employment issues at a national level. However, three issues were identified for Carers UK to address, namely

- influencing the improvement of local alternative care provision
- campaigning for the right to request flexible working
- tackling the difficulty carers find in bridging the gap between benefits and paid work.

Luke Clements, in his introduction to his *Carers and their Rights* (Carers UK 2005), made a challenging statement about this Act. He wrote:

> 'The Carers (Equal Opportunities) Act 2004 introduces an important new dimension to carers' support services, not least in seeking to assist those carers who wish to work or who wish to access education, training or leisure activities.

The new Act marks a major cultural shift in the way carers are viewed: a shift in seeing carers not so much as unpaid providers of care services for disabled people, but as people in their own right: people with the right to work, like everyone else: people who have too often been socially excluded and (like the disabled people for whom they care) often denied the life chances that are available to other people. The depth of these difficulties can be highlighted by three simple statistics:

Carers lose an average of £9,000 pa by taking on significant caring responsibilities

Over half of all carers have a caring related health condition

Carers represent one of the most socially excluded groups of people – for whom the Government's inclusion policy appears (to date) to have failed.

The 2004 Act, accordingly, requires social and health care professionals to reorientate their approach to carers. It is an Act that will, in time bring about a major cultural change in relation to such perceptions. In due course it will need to be strengthened by more robust legislation: legislation to outlaw discrimination against carers and legislation imposing specific responsibilities on the NHS to promote the health and well-being of carers.'

Carers UK has in its 2005 *Agenda for Change* risen to this challenge as well as to the conclusions in the ACE evaluation. Funding was secured for ACE 2 and it formally began in May 2005. At the Party conferences in the autumn of 2006 Carers UK put carers and work at the forefront of its presentations. It launched a new report complied by ACE National and Sheffield Hallam University, *Statistical Analysis; Working Carers: Evidence from the 2001 Census*. This was in effect an appendix to the *Who Cares Wins* report mentioned above. The report with its executive summary, *More than a Job*, received wide coverage. In essence the analysis showed that as far as employment was concerned there was a glass ceiling for carers. They were less qualified than other people in employment, more clustered in lower level jobs, had less access to higher level positions, men with heavy caring roles were less likely to be working in the financial sector and women with heavy caring roles were more concerned in wholesale/retail, hotels and catering and manufacturing sectors than other women. A particularly striking finding was that young Bangladeshi and Pakistani men and women were three times more likely than other young people to combine paid work and caring.

The challenges and complexities of work and caring were further analysed in relation to parents of sick or disabled children in a report published in November 2006, *Caring for Sick or Disabled Children: Parents' experiences of combining work and care.* Contact a Family had joined with Carers UK, ACE National and Hallam University to produce this report. For the parents, work provided both income and a chance to have part of their life away from caring. However, caring had an adverse impact on their career. Work patterns had to change or new jobs found. Flexible working and supportive managers were essential but these conditions were not universally found, and disrespect or hostility could be experienced. Incidentally the Work and Families Act 2006 will give carers the right to request flexible working but, like many newly acquired rights, the implementation may require a secondary battle.

The reports which build on data not previously available have underpinned Carers UK's focus on an equality agenda. Carers are discriminated against on many of the equality strands. The campaigning around equality issues involves other organisations being brought alongside such as Stonewall, the Disability Rights Commission and the Commission for Equality and Human Rights. But, as I have indicated in the early history, working in alliances with others has been a core reason for the success of the movement and so it remains and indeed needs to do so.

ALLIANCES

Jill Pitkeathley reported in November 1993 that she represented CNA on 19 committees and working groups. In 2001 CNA was continuing to convene and support four networks: UK Carers' Alliance, Young Carers' Alliance, Patients Forum and Employment Advisory Committee. The ACE National project was a master class in partnerships, including one with F&M Power in Austria, which was working with parents returning to the labour market. Initiating or joining alliances and partnerships was key to the carers' work. Jill Pitkeathley said in her NZ address, referred to earlier, 'disunity was never an option'. Divisions are soon exploited by politicians and funders. But working with others requires negotiation and compromise. Carers' manifestos produced by CNA were not always as forceful as some would have liked but when produced, especially at election time, they were the agreed statement of many organisations, and the more powerful because of that. One only has to envisage the alternative – a range of differing carers' manifestos with many of the differences probably incomprehensible to the outsider.

The challenges of working in alliances should not be underestimated. In March 2006 the Government announced changes to its controversial Mental Health Bill. The Mental Health Alliance had been campaigning for major changes to this bill. But for some members, as reported in the Guardian of 29 March 2006, it was a 'case of one step forward, two steps back' with 'many of the most problematic elements of the bill still being taken forward'. One Director of a mental health voluntary organisation said that 'almost everything the alliance wanted in the bill has been ditched'.

Given the carers' history of alliances it is not surprising that objective five in the Strategy Plan 2005-8 reads: 'Carers UK will continue to work collaboratively with all people and organisations who have a role to play in achieving greater recognition and equality for carers.'

SERVICE PROVISION

The time and effort given to much of the above is awesome but only becomes possible when the direct service provision is limited. Service provision has always been secondary to the policy and campaigning role and this has been a great strength. I know from personal experience how hard it is to move a service-driven organisation into one where serious time and attention is given to the social policy issues. For the carers' movement there has never been a belittling of the more direct services, but they have not been seen as paramount. Some carers' organisations have taken the opposite route, such as the Princess Royal Trust for Carers, formed in 1991, and which now runs 122 centres across the UK, employing 1,500 staff. It provides information, advice and support each year to 180,000 carers. Clearly this is a very different approach to that of Carers UK. It is no coincidence, however, that most campaigning bodies are relatively small and in effect 'punch above their weight'. Managing hundreds of staff does not give the space to devote months of senior staff time and resources to lobbying and supporting a Private Member's Bill. I recall a Child Poverty Action Group meeting in the 1970s when the Secretary of State at the DHSS said the public could be forgiven for thinking that CPAG had more staff than the Department!

In 1993 CNA discussed the provision of a freephone carers helpline and 1995 was planned as the start date. Unfortunately funding was not secured and the CarersLine did not open until 1997. However it is fair to say that between 1992 to 1997 the telephone advice and information service was improved. Clear distinctions were made between advice as opposed to information, with CAB-trained staff being employed who could provide detailed generalist advice on a range of issues. Quality advice and information was viewed as very important.

Since then the telephone helpline has had a chequered history and obtaining funding for the four full time staff needed has not usually been achieved. No one has doubted the need for such a line and in the 2006 White Paper, *Our health, our care, our say* there is a pledge to fund a national carers helpline. It says 'we will establish an information service/helpline for carers, perhaps run by a voluntary organisation' (para 5.53). Carers UK currently has some 700 calls a month and sends out a similar number of information packs. With four full time advisers in 2002-3 it received 38,982 calls in six months but was only able to respond to 19% of them. There are, of course, other sources of advice such as carers centres but these are not evenly spread across the whole of the UK. The Carers UK website is also a valuable source of information and in early 2004 there were over 14,000 website visitors a month. However, with six million carers and rising, a quantum leap forward is clearly required and the Government White Paper heralds that. Carers UK and its predecessors have struggled to maintain this kind of service and even if it had been given a much higher priority, funds still have to be found for it and then it has to be set alongside the benefits from the campaigning achievements for a huge number of unknown carers. With the growth of services for carers in statutory authorities and other voluntary bodies the provision of training has become a valued part of Carers UK activities. When the Association received its first training grant in 1990 it was to train carers. But since 1995 the training has concentrated on courses aimed at fellow professionals. The current target is to have 650 people a year attend the courses.

KEEPING CARERS INVOLVED

The absence of a major emphasis on direct services and the priority given to the research, lobbying and campaigning could have led to the carers' movement becoming a powerful campaigning body, but increasingly distant from the carers themselves. Fortunately from the outset Mary Webster and her successors made quite specific and deliberate efforts to ensure that the carers not only benefited from the outcomes of the successful campaigns but also contributed to them. One recalls the early members of the Council being urged to write to their MPs. The Association had lists of members willing to talk to the media on the issues affecting carers and the need for changes. Carers groups have always provided evidence for lobbying and data for the researchers. However over the years the needs of carers have been shown to be more varied and complex than first thought, so the response to them has resulted in more laws and policies, though these are not always known about or readily understood. So it was that during 2005 members expressed a wish to be better informed and empowered locally so that they could themselves fight for the service improvements that are still so badly needed. By November 2005 the Equal Partners project had been launched with substantial funding from the Big Lottery matched from other sources including ACE National.

Equal Partners aims to establish a powerful partnership between the national organisation and carers locally. It is to help carers make their voice heard and improve local services. The project will give carers the facts, skills and back-up to achieve change locally and in turn Carers UK will be given the evidence to strengthen its national campaigns. Carers locally will be provided with training as well as information so that with greater confidence they can tackle the local service providers. The first two newsletters in June and September 2006 summarised the key facts on such issues as rights at work and the Human Rights Act. More detailed briefing papers have been published on carers' human rights and carers and emergencies. By the end of 2006 a total of 1300 carers and carers groups had joined Equal Partners. The flow of experience that this project can provide has huge significance for as Imelda Redmond, Carers UK's Chief Executive, recognises, Government needs to know if its laws and policies are not truly improving the lives of carers and Equal Partners can do just that.

The analysis that I have tried to give as to why the carers' movement has been so successful only finally makes sense if one considers the elusive factor of leadership.

LEADERSHIP

While it is the Director's or Chief Executive's names which feature most in the press, the minutes, the reports and the correspondence, they are not acting alone. Before reflecting on the quality of the leadership since the very beginning I want briefly to put that leadership in context.

One of the most damaging events in an organisation is if the Chair and the Chief Executive fall out. The relationship between the two is vital to the health and well being of the body as a whole. The first Chair of the Council bequeathed a fine tradition in that role and the working relationship between the two key posts has overall continued to be healthy. That does not mean agreement on every issue with one or the other always having his or her way, but that ultimately they work together for the good of the organisation. Staff and committee members play their part too, but an imbalance between the two 'top' roles soon permeates the organisation and lowers morale and can reduce effectiveness.

Alliances, as I have noted, have been an essential part of the overall success and the Directors have over the years greatly benefited from the peer support. Judith Oliver made particular mention of this when I interviewed her. The Directors of such charities as the Alzheimer's Society and Contact a Family were often mentioned in the context of joint work and the Carers Alliance in particular. Good personal working relationships with peers can be underrated as a part of the success story but working in isolation is a hard and often unproductive road. Joining working groups (not necessarily the 19 of Jill Pitkeathley!) has benefits that are personal as well as organisational.

The external political environment has, again, already been referred to but merits further mention. Names crop up from Margaret Herbison in the 1960s (and of course Sir Keith Joseph) through Virginia Bottomley, Tony Newton to Tony Blair and includes both main political parties. These and others are seen as helpful and 'doers'. The three MPs who sponsored Private Members' Bills played an immensely important role at key moments. Francine Bates came to CNA in 1990 as Deputy Director having been previously campaigning for homeless people, and experienced quite a culture shock in going from the 'undeserving' to the 'deserving'. The power of the carers' argument may well have been overwhelming but it still requires politicians to support and implement what is necessary to make the tangible improvements to carers' lives.

Let me, then, discuss the Directors themselves. I once returned to an organisation I had founded and which had gone on to great things, only to be met with 'sorry, who are you?' It should happen to us all, for we make our contribution and time moves on, and the present should not be overburdened by past personalities, though the history should be known and understood. The names of three past Directors feature prominently, one solely in the records and the other two in records and in personal recollections and who shared the platform at the 40th anniversary AGM in 2005.

Roxanne Arnold has been little mentioned in the histories to date, not least because her early period as Director overlapped with the founder, Mary Webster, who was the humane inspiration that provided the momentum in the 1960s. The vision and insight of Mary Webster is nowhere better illustrated than in the first Director she helped appoint, possessing as Miss Arnold did the legal, fiscal and campaigning skills so essential at the outset. It was a quietly effective leadership backed by an extraordinarily strong committee of management.

The two past Directors most associated with the movement from 1980 are Judith Oliver and Jill Pitkeathley. Interestingly, as founder of the Association, Judith Oliver says that in 1986 she became aware of the 'founder syndrome' and felt she had to leave. Certainly organisations have suffered from dominant founders who have stayed on far too long and usually organisations suffer and take a long time to recover. The Directors were very different in style and temperament but to this outsider at this distance they brought what was absolutely necessary at the time. Both believed passionately that the issue of carers was one whose time had come and that tide of interest had to be harnessed. They were indefatigable in doing just that, their Directors' reports on activities and engagements undertaken make exhausting reading. Seizing opportunities was a hallmark of both of them, not to the extent of taking the organisation off course but in making sure that no one else ever lost sight of carers as a concern. I was not able to find any record of committee discussion about priorities until the early 1990s, suggesting that it was almost too risky to say 'no' to anything. As we shall see, this did have an impact on staff. Both created a phenomenal amount of media coverage and were willing to talk to the media. Both led their organisations in ways that had staff pleased to be there, not seeking a way out. Neither, though, was really able to achieve a clear working relationship between the national organisation and its branches and individual members.

Appointing good directors is not luck, but to succeed they need an element of good fortune. When Imelda Redmond became Director in 2003 it was at a time of ill fortune, with Carers UK facing a very serious financial crisis. With committee support she has pulled the organisation around and the current level of work and vision for the future show that strong leadership is again to the fore. With the challenge of the White Paper, *Our health, our care, our say* allied to the demographics, it will be needed. The former proposes a new deal for carers: the Government will update and extend the Prime Minister's 1999 Strategy for Carers and encourage Councils and PCTs to nominate leads for carers' services; it will establish a helpline; in each council area it will ensure that short-term, home-based respite care is established for carers in crisis or emergency situations; it will allocate specific funding for the creation of an Expert Carers programme. To hold the Government to that agenda will require all Carers UK's leadership and lobbying skills.

Just as I was finishing this history, hard evidence of the impact of the movement, that Mary Webster could only have dreamed of, and which also provided fresh challenges for Carers UK, came with the publication in May 2006 of the Government White Paper, *Security in Retirement: towards a new pensions system*. The potential and actual poverty of carers has been an argument advanced from the very beginning; all funding applications in the early years highlighted this issue. Years spent caring reduce work opportunities and with that goes loss of pension provision. Government now was meeting this concern head on. In paragraph 16 of the executive summary it states 'we recognise the value of the service that carers, both of children and of people with disabilities, contribute to society' and goes on to acknowledge how people 'mix periods of work, caring and studying during the course of their lives'. There is no equivocation: ' the current system is unfair to those with caring responsibilities, who tend to be women...'

Proposals in the White Paper to improve the position of carers include giving, as from 2010, an entitlement to a full State Pension to those who have worked or cared for 30 years. A new Carer's Credit is to be included in the Basic State Pension and the State Second Pension for those undertaking care for the sick and severely disabled for 20 or more hours a week. There is a reinforcement of the value of flexible working practices. A Pensions Bill is now in the offing, demonstrating that Government has started to take the steps to understanding that the pensions system does not fit around carers' lives. That caring impacts on pensions is now accepted. I can only give a flavour of the White Paper but in the historical context of the carers' movement any committee over the past 40 plus years would justifiably be noting in its minutes a huge sense of achievement. They would not over indulge themselves, as there is still much to do.

In this account I have tried to tease out what I see as the underlying reasons for the strength of the carers' movement. But nothing is without flaws and in the next chapter I will endeavour to discuss what seem to be some of the shortfalls, a term I prefer to failures or even mistakes. Then I will examine the impact of devolution, then finally draw some conclusions with an eye to the future.

IX

Shortfalls

Three areas merit discussion as being aspects of the movement where progress was not as evident as perhaps it should have been. The situation in 2006 is less troubling but it would be a false history not to raise these three issues, namely equal opportunities, the relationship with the disability movement and the demands made on staff at critical times.

EQUAL OPPORTUNITIES

As we have seen, the 2004 Act addressed the question of equal opportunities for carers in comparison with the population as a whole. Here I am discussing the narrower issue of equal opportunities within the carers' organisations themselves. In the 1970s and 1980s many organisations grappled with the implementation of equal opportunity policies in order to ensure that their staff and committee recruitment procedures were not inadvertently (the kindest word) excluding, say, black people, that services were truly available to all and in fact reaching them. For some organisations, the discussion and introduction of such policies was a tense and challenging time. I speak from personal experience. Many groups simply did not know how many of their users were, say, from black and minority ethnic populations and were resistant to any form of monitoring to find out. The nervousness over monitoring added to the difficulty in making a significant breakthrough. Equal opportunities soon came to embrace people with disabilities, and gays and lesbians. What happened in the carers' movement?

In 1985 the Power Report had indicated that the branches of the Council often had a majority of former carers and, by implication, were not as open to new carers as should have been the case. It was highly unlikely therefore that carers from black and minority ethnic communities would have found their way to those branches. Jill Pitkeathley does regard the early failure to attract minority ethnic carers as one of the historical mistakes of the movement.

This issue was, in fact, first raised by the staff in April 1989. This was quite late compared with many voluntary bodies but, it has to be said, not as late as some others. There had been some awareness earlier about the special needs of rural carers and, of course, young carers, but I can find no prior record of any formal discussion of equal opportunities. This late start is not surprising. The Council's concern had been single women, often middle aged or elderly, and this was a relatively homogeneous group. The Association was overwhelmed from day one and faced with enormous pressures so that taking on board an equal opportunities policy was unlikely to be a priority. Funders then, unlike today, rarely required sight of an equal opportunities policy. At that time establishing a new organisation had enough challenges without taking on 'extras'. That would not be true today. I know that as the first Director of the Alcohol Recovery Project (1966-75) we only had two black users. Now it has projects specifically for black drinkers. In 40 years the demographics of ethnicity have changed dramatically, as well as awareness of disability and sexuality. Progress has been made but never at the speed those directly affected would like.

None of this should be taken to mean that there was no mention of or concern about carers from the black and minority communities. For example, the unit at the King's Fund had, in 1986, paid attention to ethnic minority considerations in the informal caring programme. As we saw, the 1990 Social Services Inspectorate report also highlighted the needs of minority carers. Of special interest is the account published in 1997 of the Bury Carers Helpline, by Sandra Leventon and Lucette Tucker, as the service included a helpline for the Muslim community. But these were all separate initiatives and not part of any sustained strategy.

With the stability of the merger came, in 1989, the matter of equal opportunities. A policy was formulated and adopted in May 1990. But having a policy is the easier part, as the staff realised. In October 1990 the staff asked the management committee to consider the following resolution: 'staff unanimously propose that the management committee make equal opportunities a priority. We need to look at improving the Association's accessibility to carers from all sectors of the community and then take real steps towards combating discrimination.' A working group of two staff and two committee members was appointed 'to take the matter forward'. In November 1991 the third draft of a code of practice was agreed by the management committee. The focus was on the carers and six groups of carers were identified as not being reached. They were:

- Carers who were economically disadvantaged
- Carers from black and minority ethnic communities
- Carers in the rural areas
- Carers who themselves had mental health difficulties, or were physically disabled including the frail elderly
- Young carers
- Gay and lesbian carers.

In April 1993 the committee received a report from the All Carers Coordinating Group which, on its own admission, had not met 'for some considerable time'. It reviewed progress to date, noting that there had been discussion papers on minority ethnic carers, carers with disabilities, young carers and 'poor' carers. There had been training for staff and the Association's 'image' with regard to its journal, *The Carer*, and its Annual Report was thought to 'have improved significantly'. Much more, however, needed to be done with regard to the branches' policies and practices. Apart from young carers, there was little targeting of excluded carer groups and no specific funding made available. It was not surprising, therefore, in July 1995 to find that there was concern that groups of carers were still not being reached 'for example black, disabled, gay and lesbian and economically disadvantaged'.

The publicly expressed intentions were there. In the 1994-98 Strategy Plan there is clear reference to equal opportunities policies with regard to employment of staff. Within the plans to set up regional offices, priority is to be given to projects for minority ethnic carers and rural carers. In 1996 £9,000 was spent on translating two key booklets into 10 languages. Delivering practical projects to meet the needs of minority ethnic carers was, however, more taxing than translations. The experience of the City Parochial Foundation (CPF) is instructive.

From 1992-7 the CPF gave £1.5 million to fund 11 voluntary sector carers' projects in London. This arose from its own research in 1991 which had looked at the needs of 300 carers in four London boroughs. The important finding in this context was that services were consistently under used by minority ethnic carers. Of the 11 projects funded, three focused exclusively on minority ethnic carers and two had posts addressing the needs of Asian carers. Although, overall, much that was positive came out of the scheme, one conclusion is highly relevant. 'The three-year funding period, enlightened compared to year-by-year funding, was still found to be too short for some time consuming development work. It ignores the necessity to set the work up, which in all cases took a period of one to two years. Five years therefore allows three years of developmental working time, and with particularly exacting work, such as access work with hard-to-reach minority ethnic communities, even ten years may be more realistic.'

It is therefore understandable that CNA did not establish nationally or through its branches a range of projects to draw in the hard-to-reach carers. Hidden carers had, after all, been a concern since 1989, even without the consideration of equal opportunities.

By 1997 the equal opportunities sub-committee was turning its attention to the management committee itself. It said that more effort should be made to recruit black committee members. It repeated this concern in November 1998, though recognised that in order to do this it needed, as an organisation, to broaden its membership base, certainly if tokenism was to be avoided.

By the late 1990s the National Black Carers Network was established. Was that development a sign that CNA had failed in its attempts to draw in black and minority ethnic carers? The answer is, in truth, 'yes, but'. All minority groups over the past 20 to 30 years have taken the view that they need to work from their own base to ensure that the mainstream services are responsive to their particular requirements. Setting up their own organisations, small or large, has been part of that process. London has been particular witness to this, with refugee community groups and supplementary and mother tongue schools, for example. As the black population aged so black elderly groups formed, not as a condemnation of, say, Age Concern but because they reasoned that they knew their needs better and could address them in ways that were more culturally appropriate.

In 1996 a Cancer Black Care Support Group was formed in London. This group first came together in response to a growing concern that black people were not accessing appropriate intervention and treatments in time because of the stigma and fear associated with the disease. Despite the development of research and treatment in this area, amongst the black community there remained a lack of understanding about the effects of cancer. In addition health care provision for cancer sufferers has not always been sensitive to the particular needs of people from the black community.

The Black Carers Network has worked closely with Carers UK, especially in London, through Carers London (part of Carers UK). For instance, a joint conference was organised in June 2004 with the theme 'Raising awareness of black carers' issues in Primary Health Care'. Carers London meets quarterly with its networks including the London Black Carers Workers network. In 2005 during Carers Week there was a conference for 180 black and minority ethnic participants on 'Opportunities in Employment, Learning and Leisure for BME Carers'. They also worked with the Chinese Carers Support Group to run an event for 70 participants. A valuable new publication, *Balancing Life and Caring*, was translated into six languages in 2005.

Given the track record in research and the telling ways in which case histories have been used, the Equal Opportunities and Membership sub-committee said in January 2000 that the organisation should draw much more on the range of caring experiences which would provide good case histories and different perspectives. It mentioned 'mental health and alcohol abuse'. Incidentally the latter is the sole reference I have found to caring where alcohol abuse is involved.

The 2001 Census provided for the first time information on carers within the minority communities. For example, among working age people caring varies by ethnicity. Among men the Indian, Pakistani, Bangladeshi and White British groups are most likely to be carers –

about 11-12% for each group. Among women the Pakistani, Bangladeshi and White British groups report the most caring – 15 to 16% of these women are carers. There are also significant percentages among the Irish (9%), Indian (12%) and Black Caribbean (8%) women.

We have noted earlier in this history the economic and health impact on carers, much of which was given statistical confirmation by the 2001 Census. To date I have not seen any specific data or projects relating to gay and lesbian carers. Obviously the legislation is aimed at all, but all have to know about it to access the services and the benefits. The value base of Carers UK is forthright, as set out in the 2005-8 Strategy: 'We have a strong commitment to equality of opportunity – campaigning for equality for all carers, valuing the contribution and richness that comes from having a diverse membership base.' Membership per se is, as we have seen, a tough challenge in itself. Collaborating with others is also part of the value base. Together with the relevant minority agencies and networks and with such a strong campaigning focus to secure benefits for all, carers from all backgrounds should stand to gain, indeed must.

RELATIONSHIP WITH THE DISABILITY MOVEMENT

I have already, in chapter VII, discussed the tension between the carer and disability movements. There is certainly one view that more could have been done from the carers' side to reduce the gap in understanding between the two sides. It is, however, the case that in all carer campaigns there were some disability organisations and on some issues the disability lobby was divided within itself. There was not, for example, universal support from the disability lobby for the Carers (Equal Opportunities) Act 2004 though the Act emphasised the needs of carers outside the caring role. There is now, however, more dialogue with the radical disability movement for which this Act has been a spur.

There is an ideological difference that can be powerfully stated, namely that carers prop up the system, that support for carers sterotypes women and reinforces discrimination against disabled people. If the cared for had all the necessary services then carers would be free to live their own lives. Reading any carer case history it is hard to imagine that the carer would not welcome better services to help the cared for person. Improved services are in everyone's interests. This does not of course rule out any carer wanting to have that role as an essential part of their relationship with the disabled person. But clinging to the role when help might have been available does create the situation that feeds the case advanced by the disability groups. For example, the carer who did not take a holiday for ten years and said 'I would not want anyone to say that I had not done my job' is in danger of unnecessarily confirming the worst fears of the disability lobby.

Imelda Redmond believes that the Human Rights Act 1998 provides the potential for the two movements to develop common interests. For example, case law indicates that it can be a violation of someone's human rights if they are treated differently because of their situation; and yet a carer awaiting surgery for a serious back problem was forced to continue to help her daughter shower after the local authority withdrew two care staff who had previously provided help (an assessment said it was too risky for the health of their backs). An adapted shower would have helped, but the waiting list was a year long. Here there is common interest in challenging poor practice and restrictive attitudes to health and safety that do not adequately consider service users' rights. More generally Carers UK argues in its report, *Whose rights are they anyway? Carers and the Human Rights Act*, that the Act has not yet been of value to carers.

The report published in March 2006 states: 'The Human Rights Act (HRA) offers a unique framework which could be used by policy makers and service providers. This framework, of balancing different or competing rights against each other, and against the interests of the wider community, is particularly relevant to carers. This is because the rights of the carer will always need to be balanced against the right of the person who receives care or support. Disabled people, in particular, have fought a long battle to have their right to independence recognised and respected, and to ensure that they can claim their human rights, including rights to make decisions about their own lives. Carers UK wholeheartedly supports this change. Carers UK seeks to ensure that carers, too, are treated with the dignity and respect that all human beings deserve. The HRA, with its framework of balancing rights has a significant contribution to make to this debate.'

There is also the issue of resources. The above report found that 'resources are inadequate to allow rights to be protected'. The White Paper on health and social care, to which reference has already been made, raised a lot of hopes about the strengthening of community based services. Professor Peter Beresford said on publication there will need to be increased priority and funding for social care. 'Carry on campaigning looks like being the watchword if we are to get the best from this brave new package.' By March 16th 2006 the Guardian was reporting that 'four in five local authorities are moving to tighten the eligibility rules for services for elderly and disabled people, in response to a record £1.8 billion gap in funding for social care and the knock-on effects of the cash crisis in the NHS. The trend, which implies that 70% of councils will now offer services only to people whose needs are adjudged 'critical' or 'substantial', raises grave doubts about the Government's ambition to achieve a shift in health and social care provision towards a preventive agenda, as outlined in a white paper in January.' If the resources crisis unfolds in the way that now seems possible then the closer the relationship between the two movements the better; more than that, it will be essential.

STAFF OVERLOAD

It is not my experience that staff in the voluntary sector ever feel that they are underemployed. Tough working hours, with or without time off in lieu, are common. Even within that context there has been a recurrent theme in the movement of stress on the staff. I have referred earlier to the staff in the Association writing to the management committee in October 1986 to say how overworked and stressed they were to the extent of 'dreading the next phone call'. In 1990 the Director, Jill Pitkeathley, reported to the committee that 'we were at a very difficult stage of growth – the victims of our own success – because the profile of the organisation had been raised, increasing demands and expectations were being put on the staff'. Earlier that year the 'emotional' pressure on branches had also been a cause for concern.

In March 1999 the acting Chief Executive, Francine Bates, had at the request of the Board produced a report, in conjunction with the senior management team, on the core functions of CNA. In that report Francine made an analysis of the staff position which is worth quoting in full.

'It is fair to say that in the last 10 years CNA took advantage of virtually every opportunity to promote the cause of carers and the work of the organisation, often at considerable costs to staff and volunteers who have devoted time and energy, often above the call of duty, eg working long hours and at weekends.

Perhaps it would be helpful to draw an analogy between CNA and being a full-time carer. As an organisation, we are constantly on duty, responding to demands that are placed on us with very little respite. Increasingly as staff and branch volunteers, we are facing mounting pressures and are expected to do more, despite a lack of adequate resources.

The senior management team are concerned that CNA is in danger of becoming a victim of our own success – 'a super carer'. As we all know too well – this can lead to burn out and collapse. We feel that most staff and possibly some of our branch activists are now up to capacity in terms of what they can take on. However, the 'outside world', for example the media, policy makers, voluntary organisations, carers' workers and indeed carers have a perception that CNA is a 'huge' organisation with large numbers of paid staff. We have often wrongly been compared with organisations such as Age Concern or Help The Aged – both of which have more staff in their fund-raising departments between them than our entire paid workforce.

Against this background, CNA may find it hard to respond to the announcement of the National Carers Strategy which has considerable implications for our future work. Given the rapid development of other charities in the carers' field, CNA needs to consider reviewing and redefining our position.'

Needless to say CNA did respond rapidly to the National Carers Strategy, but that required a huge effort and does not detract from the thrust of the argument. It shows how hard it is to break away from the 'super carer' role either as a person or an organisation.

The Strategy 2000-3 made no reference to staff. In the Strategy for 2005-8 under Objective 4, Governance and Management, the welcome statement is made that part of the objective is to be 'a good employer that values the staff and respects their role and contribution, there will be:

- Regular reviews of personnel policies
- A staff development plan
- Regular reviews of terms and conditions of employment'.

Some of this may have been implicit before, but the explicit commitment in the strategy plan gives all concerned a benchmark. Reports of overworked or stressed staff in the future, should they occur, will now have a context in which to consider any such problem.

These three issues are what struck me in tracking the movement over 40 years or more. Of course there would have been other matters that were not handled well but many of these would have been the norm for any developing charity. A Board development day in December 2001 raised a host of interesting concerns but I can think of no charity Board that would not have felt a great sense of familiarity with them. The carers' movement is of interest because it has not been blown off course by the normal trials and tribulations of governance and management.

Even a moderately sensitive reader north of the border might by now have said 'this is all about England, I haven't read one reference to Scotland, let alone Wales or Northern Ireland'. They would be right. Devolution came late on in the carers' history but needs discussing.

X

Devolution

Before too long it will certainly be necessary to write histories of the work of Carers UK in Scotland, Wales and Northern Ireland to take account of the particular circumstances in each of those countries and the key personalities involved. As an illustration, the scope and depth of work undertaken in Scotland is set out in the Appendix. I will attempt just to see how devolution impacted on CNA and then indicate how the style of the organisation was translated to other parts.

Knowing in 1997 the intentions of the newly elected Labour Government with regard to devolution, the CNA AGM created a devolution sub-committee which by 2000 had become a devolution and constitution committee. The 2000-3 Strategy was aware of the work which would now need to be undertaken through 'devolved assemblies and parliaments', which had been established in 1999. In 2001 CNA changed its name to Carers UK, better to reflect that it was a membership organisation. At the same time the nation offices changed their names to Carers Scotland, Carers Wales and Carers Northern Ireland. From July 2001 the Chief Executive's reports to the UK Board included separate sections on the activities of the three countries and it is from these reports and the minutes of the three countries that my comments are drawn.

What emerges immediately is how the tried and tested ways of working are quickly in place in the home countries. Some very familiar problems, too, appear, such as the work pressures on branches or the difficulty in attracting new members or committee members into the branches. For example, the Carers Scotland Committee in June 2004 said it needed a broader membership base than at present; it had been in decline since 2000. Issues relating to membership such as fees, benefits and involvement were discussed. Mary Webster would have listened with interest. In 2003 Carers Wales was discussing ways of reaching the 'hidden' carers, a problem first considered in 1989. In NI social workers in some areas were expressing concerns that carers' assessments were raising carers' expectations without the resources to meet them. The Chief Executive's report on the three countries in July 2001 showed how soon carers' concerns were on the various agendas.

In Northern Ireland there had been a very successful launch of the publication, *Training for Carers in Northern Ireland – Issues and Opportunities*. The Carers Strategy Reference Group made up of carers and carers' organisations had submitted the Carers Strategy for NI to the Departmant of Health, Social Services and Public Safety. Consultation on the Carers and Disabled Children's Bill had taken place and the issue of young carers had been highlighted. The Review of Community Care in NI was underway and a member of the Carers NI committee was on the Project board for the review. Carers NI had already submitted preliminary evidence, including a Carers Manifesto for NI. Six briefing sessions had been run for carers groups on the new public health strategy in NI. There was a duty on public bodies in NI to promote equal opportunities for 'persons with dependants' and Carers NI had run very well received 'tools for change' sessions on this duty. Then with Mencap it had produced a 'Tools for Change' pack for the use of their own groups. The momentum of this publicly visible work is remarkable.

Carers Scotland was no different. It was active in speaking at meetings and conferences to discuss the Scottish Carers Legislation which had a four month consultation period. Draft national care standards were issued and Carers Scotland was assisting in formulating the response to this draft. It was a member of the Care Home working group responding to the consultation paper, Future of Scottish Homes. Research was done with Crossroads Scotland on hospital discharges and this was published in Carers Week. Two debates on carers' issues had taken place in the Scottish Parliament with a number of references to Carers Scotland. Again the organisation was a member of the short life working group on proposals to change the Mental Health (Scotland) Act 1984 which will aim to include new legislation to consider the role of carers. It was also a member of the Chief Medical Officer's Expert Group on the health care of older people. A Carers' Manifesto had been produced for Scotland for the UK general election and a conference on long term care organised with two other bodies. In February 2006 the Scottish Executive published a seminal report, *The Future of Unpaid Care in Scotland*, and followed this up in April with the Directorate of Primary and Community Care in the Health Department issuing *NHS Carer Information Strategies; Minimum requirements and Guidance on Implememtation*. Analysis and implementation were going hand in hand.

In the run-up to devolution and on behalf of the Welsh Office, Carers Wales organised a major consultation on the needs of carers. It also developed a Carers Manifesto which was used widely with the candidates for the new Assembly. It was also closely involved in working with the officials in drafting the Wales Carers Strategy which was launched in 2000 and was represented on the Carers Strategy Review Panel to review its implementation and future development. Carers Wales was also on the reference group for the Assembly's research project on young carers. It was involved in a whole series of Assembly working groups, including the working group on Patient

Support and Advocacy in the NHS and in the development of the Wales NSF for Older People. It held high profile events such as the launch of the Carers UK publication, *You Can Take Him Home Now*; a major conference on Carers and Employment in 2005 and organised the 'Carers Summit' in 2006 on behalf of the Welsh Assembly Government to launch the Carers Equal Opportunities Act. When the NHS in Wales was re-organised in 2003, Carers Wales successfully lobbied for a carer member to be appointed to each of the new Local Health Boards.

In 2006, with Dr Hywel Francis MP, it successfully lobbied for the first ever Cabinet level 'Carers Champion' in the Welsh Assembly Government.

Finally it was involved in developing and supporting key partnerships: the Wales Carers Alliance, the Wales Carers' Workers Network, the Young Carers' Workers Network, the network to support the carer members on the Local Health Boards and the Carers and Employment Forum.

In all three countries there was a surge and breadth of activity that echoed so intriguingly the initial years of the Council in the 1960s. All the characteristics were there: the action research, the alliances with other like minded bodies, the lobbying, the publications, the direct engagement of the carers themselves, the wider involvement of the committee members, the conferences and, supremely, the all-embracing nature of the work. Nothing of relevance to carers escaped their eagle eyes. They were also well placed to be the platform for launching the publications of Carers UK. And so it has continued during these first years of devolution. It would be somewhat tedious to list all the home country achievements over these five years but the examples above should convey the flavour of it all. Let me conclude with one final example from each of the countries to show how the carers' movement has rooted itself so firmly in new soils.

In 2003 the elections for the National Assembly in Wales resulted in a Labour majority of one rather than a coalition as previously. Carers Wales had to adapt to this new political situation. 'In the first Assembly term, much of the health and social services agenda was governed by consensus working. There already appears to be a different, more challenging approach from the opposition parties. This will give us new opportunities to lobby and influence Assembly members of all parties and ensure they are aware of carers' concerns and issues. We have already met with some of the new members and, with the Wales Carers Alliance, held a cross party briefing seminar. Assembly members have asked us to hold these at regular intervals and also to send them regular briefing bulletins. We are also meeting with the newly created Minister for Social Justice and Regeneration to emphasise the equality and social inclusion agenda for carers.'

In 2005 'Carers Northern Ireland spearheaded a submission to the First and Deputy First Minister on the Green Paper on a Single Equality Bill for Northern Ireland. Other key bodies, including the Equality Commission, support our position on the inclusion of carers within a Single Equality Bill'.

In August 2005 Carers Scotland reported that its 'ACE (Action for Carers and Employment) policy and development officer is now in place and making good contacts. Two local authorities have confirmed interest in working with Carers Scotland to develop a flexible working policy for carers. This may lead the way for other local authorities to come on board.'

It is worth noting that the recent project, Equal Partners, to which I referred at the end of chapter VIII, ensures in its newsletters that attention is given to the developments in all of the home countries and highlights the relevant websites and campaigning roles to be undertaken.

I know there will have been day to day organisational headaches and financial concerns but the continuing record of achievement and influence is unmistakable and is the foundation of a significant and substantial legacy for carers in the three countries.

XI

Conclusions

'The central problem is insuperable.' These are the words of the movement's first Director, Roxanne Arnold, on her retirement in August 1975. Were she to read Society Guardian for March 15th 2006 she might be tempted to reflect that her words still hold true. In the Guardian a two page feature on carers highlighted the case study of David Harkins, struggling to care for his mentally ill wife and his 15-year-old autistic son. For a few days a week he has two hours off when his wife attends a class but he has not had a night off in 18 years. Reading this wider history of the movement as a whole Miss Arnold would probably be astonished at what has been achieved and note that single women caring for their elderly parents is no longer the core concern. But David Harkins, she might argue, is as much 'under house arrest' as her single women ever were. At the Carers UK AGM in November 2005 Imelda Redmond looked forward to a time 40 years from now when 'we should be celebrating the end' with all carers 'recognised and supported', seen as true partners in any service provision and financially secure with, for example, proper pensions. So, in the cold light of day, what exactly is the success of the movement?

In this final chapter let me try to distil what I see as the evidence for the success without denying the validity of the need for another 40 years of campaigning.

We should never underestimate the isolation of carers 40 years ago, nor the public ignorance about their plight. In the 1980s it was still common, says Jill Pitkeathley, to have 'carers' changed to 'careers' by the managers of venues where CNA had booked its conferences. Demonstrating that carers are out there in great numbers is no longer necessary. In social policy terms they will never be off the agenda. That was not bound to be the case when Mary Webster began the journey.

We should also remember that in 1980 some of the doughty founders of the Council thought their job had been done. The financial position of the single woman carer had improved and much of what they had set out to do had been accomplished. But they were just looking at one tiny segment of the carers' world. It is only over time that the complexities of the seemingly straightforward term 'carer' have been uncovered. The single women were, in fact, simply the tip of the iceberg: 300,000 of them have become 6 million carers.

Challenges have been revealed as the work progressed. One recalls the first time that young carers emerged, with the letter to the Association in 1982. The work of Contact a Family highlighted the caring role of the parents of disabled children. The broader the base of the carer organisation, the more the members in the branches brought their concerns to the fore and the easier it was to research and survey the members to get the raw data for the campaigns. The General Household Surveys and the 2001 Census provided invaluable and incontrovertible national data about, for example, hours of care, the health and age of carers and the working patterns of carers. Essentially, over time it has become more complex and the 2006 Carers UK report on Carers and the Human Rights Act 1998 is a good illustration of that. Such a report also shows how Carers UK has sought to renew itself whilst not losing contact with the essentials of the historical legacy. Later I want to look forward to some of the likely future demographic changes which will add further layers to the concept of 'carer' and will certainly require Carers UK to maintain the capacity to renew itself.

Any notion of success is relative. As I said earlier, as the Council was being founded I was starting as the first Director of the Alcohol Recovery Project, as it is now called. The term in fact used in 1966 was 'alcoholics'. 'Alcoholic' went out as a term of diagnosis to be replaced by 'alcohol dependency' or 'people with drink-related problems'. I mention this personal history again because in the same *Guardian* (15 March 2006) that had *two pages* on carers there was a very brief *9 inch column* headed 'Alcohol-related illness soars as 1 in 18 addicts get treatment'. The article shows that drinking has been increasing since the 1960s and looks to continue, and despite the Government's alcohol harm reduction strategy begun in 2004 only a small proportion of those needing treatment are getting it. 8.2 million people in England have an alcohol problem, 1.3 million children are affected by their parents' alcohol problems. These figures are in some ways more challenging than the national carer statistics but over 40 years the campaigning bodies have made very little impact compared with the carers' organisations. The 'deserving' nature of the carers' cause is one reason for that, but not the sole one. The unified and collaborative campaigning focus of the movement has led, for instance, to three Acts of Parliament which began as Private Members' Bills, and that kind of evidence is what others have not been able to celebrate.

However, such triumphs as the Acts of Parliament were not seen as ends in themselves but as steps along the road where the end is not yet in sight. The carers' movement has been strong on its awareness of the gap between rhetoric and reality. It has been assiduous in its following up of the actual impact of legislation and how far community care is in fact operating as it was intended. Having a right to an assessment under an Act is one thing, claiming that right is another and receiving the support services deemed necessary after the assessment is yet another. The gap invariably centres on resources. Carers' support is valued at £57 billion per year but no such sum is simply transferred across to the statutory authorities as part of their carers' budgets. There is a constant battle for resources both within government and from outside it.

In *Society Guardian* November 23rd 2005, David Brindle analysed the resource issue for the services for those with learning disabilities. This group is now a social services responsibility having been that of the NHS. Over half the English authorities will exceed their learning disability budgets for last year. There has been a dramatic change in the demographics of this group since the NHS began to divest itself of the responsibility. 'More children are being born with multiple disabilities and are surviving into adulthood, not least in south Asian communities; learning disabled adults are, happily, living much longer and very often into old age; and people's expectations are changing – more families want their disabled children to leave home when they grow up and fewer are prepared to be carers for life.' A report commissioned by the Association of Directors of Social Services says that the way forward is to pool funding streams, reduce spending on institutional care and fund flexible and individualised support. Pilot schemes which have funded the latter show that the costs per individual can drop dramatically.

The above analysis illustrates many things, one of which is that carers' aspirations and expectations can change. In no sense is the carers' world static. There are today 6 million carers but there are new carers appearing all the time, probably 9 million by 2037, there are episodic carers, one third of carers start or cease caring in any one year, and there are groups who still may not see themselves as carers. Inevitably therefore in this changing scene there will be people who do not know they are carers with, say, a right to an assessment. As Imelda Redmond says 'we are working to benefit Mrs Smith who does not even know she is a carer'. 'There is always more to do' was one of the lessons highlighted

THE HISTORY OF THE CARERS' MOVEMENT

by Jill Pitkeathley in her address in New Zealand in 2005. Successfully applying for a major grant is wonderful for one day but then the work funded actually has to be started. Similarly, securing a national carers' strategy is both a triumph and the start of a lot more hard work. Resting on its laurels is fortunately not part of the carers' movement's psyche.

Despite the publicly recognised successes of the past 40 years there are still monumental challenges as the Carers UK *Agenda for Change* makes clear. It sets out five key changes which are needed if carers are to be given a choice about caring and the opportunity of a life outside of caring. These are worth repeating:

- Better recognition of carers
- Freedom from poverty
- Respect for carers' own health and well-being
- Real opportunities to work
- Full inclusion in all aspects of society.

If the founders of the Council in 1965 were to return, one aspect of all the developments and changes might well produce a wry sigh; namely, that women are still at the forefront of caring. Women are more likely to be carers in all age groups under 75 years. A quarter of all women aged 50-59, and about 1 in 6 men, provide unpaid care. The likelihood of being a carer is always greater for women than for men. Will it still be like that when in 2037 we have 9 million carers? This raises questions about the future and in this final section I want to give some thought to what might be some of the challenges that lie ahead. Will it be more of the same so that the future analysis of the 9 million carers just reflects pro rata the analysis of the present 6 million? Or are there any different trends that are now emerging?

The trouble with the future is that there are bound to be developments that no one could have foreseen and which may have considerable influence on the carer environment. When Jill Pitkeathley wrote her book *It's My Duty Isn't It? The Plight of Carers in Our Society* in 1989 she concluded with a look at future developments. Some were spot on, such as the impact of the divorce rate and the increasing mobility of the population on the patterns of caring. On the other hand the very positive view she took of residential homes for the elderly may now need to be tempered by the emergence of elder abuse both in homes and by professional care staff in a person's own home. This surfaced in 1993 and was discussed at CNA. It reappears as an issue on quite a regular basis. It is not that it is necessarily widespread. It doesn't need to be for people to read or see it and say 'I won't let my mother go into a home'.

The demographics hold some clues or worries for the future. Life expectancy increases all the time, so that getting to 90 is now common and 100 by no means rare. The positive side of this is the possibility for families of being able more openly to anticipate the carer role or the need to ensure that care is provided. The children faced with the caring dilemma will themselves be much older. Then, as having children later becomes much more common, the conflict between bringing up children and caring for elderly parents becomes more likely and becomes acute should one of the children be disabled. Preparing for caring seems to be a theme that could usefully form the next campaign. Without some prior discussion families can find themselves locked into sterile debates: 'I won't let you go into a Home' – 'I am not going to ruin your lives, you must find me a Home' – 'Please don't put me into one of those Homes' – 'I don't want strangers coming into my house and washing me'- and so on.

The debate above assumes a basically 'normal' family unit. Divorce and remarriage, to name but two factors, change the scenario. In your second marriage your ex-mother-in-law requires care and there is no one else but you available. Children are faced with a very ill stepfather. The permutations are endless. In such circumstances, how obligated do various 'family' members feel to take on a caring role? What does society expect? We would not defend today the understood obligation of the single daughter to give up everything to care for her parents. But in the present and future mosaic of family relationships, what is everyone expecting? If one adds to this population mobility, with children moving either to a better area or to get a job, then the caring for some is going to be very problematic. Carers UK says that 'demographic predictions make it imperative that carers are put firmly at the centre of the Government's agenda'. The data is not ambiguous.

Carers UK is right to be challenging Government, and indeed all of us, to work out how we want the care role to develop over, say, the next twenty years. The choice would appear to be simple though not easy to implement. In order to meet some of the costs of services that carers and the cared for need, if they are to have any quality of life, an increase in tax will be necessary, as resources are not being shifted across from health to social care at anything like the level necessary. Some of the proposed shifts are ambiguous as far as carers are concerned. In March 2006 the Health Secretary suggested that people suffering from asthma and heart diseases could better be cared for at home by community nurses rather than at great cost with repeated visits to hospitals. Will such a move wait until there are sufficient community care resources, or are the unpaid family carers going to find themselves in the front line?

If the above is not the answer then the policy initiatives will need to concentrate on removing the barriers that carers face in, say, seeking to combine caring responsibilities with work. We have seen how much the ACE project has achieved to date but it can only be the beginning. The benefits system and the employment procedures need to work together to ensure that caring and working is not only possible but is stress free. Ending up in distressed financial circumstances was one of the overriding fears of the single women in the 1960s and poverty and caring are still closely linked. Data from the 2001 Census gives detailed information about the geographical distribution of carers. They are not evenly spread. The pattern of caring does not fit with the geographical distribution of the over 85s. In fact it more closely resembles patterns of poor health and of socio-economic deprivation. Carers are less concentrated, for instance, in London, central and southern England compared with areas of Northern Ireland, South Wales, Cornwall and parts of northern England. Even since 2001 matters have been made worse by the uncertainties over pensions. Saving for a private pension is now recommended, occupational pension schemes are becoming a thing of the past and proposals are made to raise the retirement age. In such a context the position of the carer is highly problematic. Carers UK's *Agenda for Change* is pressing for a citizen's pension for all pensioners including carers.

We have noted how assiduous the carers' movement has been in creating alliances to bring about changes in services, benefits or legislation. New allies may be needed without jettisoning the tried and trusted. On February 11th 2006 the *Guardian* reported on what it termed the 'guerilla mothers' of disabled children. They had spent many years fighting lone battles on behalf of their disabled children with little success. Now they were joining forces to start a grassroots movement, Parents Councils. 'The aim of a council is simple – to have parents with disabled children represented at every level of decision-making in health, education and social services. Only then they believe will real changes occur.' The Leicestershire Council took five years of agitating to get established. It now has 1200 members and four funded posts. A nationwide Federation of Parents Councils will be in place by the end of

2006. The concept of 'carer' is not mentioned in the article but it is hard to imagine that an alliance here will not be of great benefit to all.

As we have already seen, the notion of carers as 'deserving' is an influential factor in the movement but that term extends, by implication, to the cared for. The elderly, ill or disabled are themselves also equally 'deserving'. The question does not so far appear to have arisen as to whether the movement can easily encompass those who care for, say, people with drinking problems. One of the leading authorities on the effects of drinking problems in the family setting is Professor Jim Orford. His recent study (along with others), *Coping with Alcohol and Drug Problems* (2005), describes how family members in Australia, England and Mexico cope with alcohol and drug problems in the family. In the 280 pages the term 'carer' is never used. Yet what these family members found most supportive would be familiar to carers:

- Emotional support
- Provision of accurate information
- Practical or material support.

Without forcing a marriage between the carer and the addiction worlds there nonetheless could be benefits to the latter if there was a dialogue between the two. There may be even more carers out there than the demographic trends suggest.

Population mobility was mentioned above but there is a wider context to that, namely the changing population brought about by the inward flow of migrants, both economic and asylum seekers, adding to the earlier immigration from the West Indies and Asia. How do the caring patterns and family expectations work out in these very diverse communities? What means are needed to reach them and ensure they have the best information available? Are there issues in some of these communities that are only now surfacing? These questions have a real practical importance when one considers that some cities, such as Leicester, are now approaching the time when there will not be a white majority population. Then for some other groups and individuals, caring at a distance is a real problem. Your mother is ill in your home country, but you cannot return without risk of imprisonment. There may be concerns for Carers UK to discuss that extend way beyond trying to ensure that carers' services are accessible and that its equal opportunities policy is sound in practice. Contact a Family, for example, is now translating materials into eastern European languages to support families who have migrated to the UK.

The United Kingdom is not, of course, the only European country with carers as an issue, both as a group requiring services here and now and as a demographic challenge. In December 2006 Eurocarers became a constituted organisation in the eyes of the European Commission. Fifteen countries are at present involved, primarily represented by carers' organisations and academics. They have come together because of increasing contact between carers' organisations across Europe and a realization that The Commission and the European Parliament have a key role in carers' lives, not least through legislation on human rights and discrimination. The demographic challenge is, for the older members of the EU, to remain competitive with an ageing population and, for the newer members, seeing their young people migrate, leaving older family members without traditional support in times of need. Carers UK is fully committed to Eurocarers, as its history would lead one to anticipate.

There can be no final word in any account of the carers' movement. Carers UK is not going to be able to say at the end of one year, 'at least next year should be easier'. If Imelda Redmond is right it will be 40 years before one of her successors can say it. A huge amount has been achieved and some of the old agendas can be ticked off. But as more data becomes available, as in the 2001 Census and other research, so the multi- faceted nature of the carers' world is made more evident. The new agenda lengthens.

From time to time modern politicians leave office in order to spend more time with their families and almost everyone applauds it (some cynically suspect the real motives). To date I have not read of someone notable leaving public life in order to be a carer, namely they *have* to spend more time with their family. Many unknown people do it. Politicians go to prison and emerge as experts and advocates of prison reform, having discovered what the voluntary organisations having been saying for years. The carer agenda might be very interesting should a male public figure 'retire' to take up the strain of a carer role. What would surprise such a person might be how modest in some ways are the requests of the carers.

Over the 40 and more years the tone of the movement has been modest. On occasion the movement has reined itself in from being too strident or unrealistic in its demands. 'I'm always surprised at how reasonable carers' requests are' said one Director. That doesn't mean to say that they and the ones they care for should not have more, but that is not how they have approached matters. The case history of David Harkins, cited above, is informative. The system has essentially failed him, yet his only complaint is that the two hours a day that his wife is taken to her classes cannot be totally relied upon and will be cancelled if staff are ill or the hall has been double booked. He says: 'They don't realise how much these couple of hours mean to me. These groups get grants, the staff are paid, so why don't they provide a structured and regular service? Is it too much to ask, just a couple of hours to recharge my batteries?' Similar case histories were published in *The Guardian* on 6th December 2006. My only cavil (or should it be more than that?) is the headline on the 6th December: 'Accidental heroes'. Apart from the absence of heroines, casting carers as heroes may lead some to applaud them but not see that what they want are services, rights and recognition rather than heroic status – no one is going to make a Hollywood epic.

In writing this history a number of people said that one of the reasons for the movement's success was that carers was an idea whose time had come, that there was a 'constellation of stars' with key factors such as the demographics making success if not inevitable then highly likely. I would rather say that there was not one constellation of stars but rather a series. I think back, for example, to perhaps the very first constellation, the meeting in 1965 at the LSE between Mary Webster and Nancy Seear. The history is littered with such critical events and we can muse on the 'what ifs' but the fact is during five decades there has been a developing movement, which still has to be sustained, that has brought immense benefits to carers.

Finally it is worth reflecting on the notion that carers were an idea or cause whose time had come. If you look at the history of other voluntary organisations that began at about the same time, namely the 1960s, many of those no doubt felt equally strongly that their time had come too. In their book *The Unsung Sixties* Helene Curtis and Mimi Sanderson interviewed 36 people involved in the founding of charities in the 1960s. By 2004, when the book was published, 34 of these organisations were still operating, including Carers UK. Some have struggled more than others. Some, like Shelter, have become household names. Some, like Mother Care for Children in Hospital (now Action for Sick Children), were able in one special area to transform all our thinking and practice. Some have battled on and maybe only now are sensing that their time has come: the Child Poverty Action Group had, in 2005, a Government pledged to end child poverty. Maybe all we can say is that they were fortunate to sense and act on the unmet need of concern to them in the 1960s and not a decade earlier.

As I commented before, success is relative and one cannot compare the history of Carers UK with, say, Shelter. There are no historic league tables. What I feel confident in stating is that whatever the zeitgeist of the times, whatever the constellation of the stars, the success of the movement to date has been built upon the skills, energy, political know-how and sheer hard work of a huge number of people. Having great ideas is fine, even fun, but it is the next step that is vital, namely finding the people to implement them. That has been the great good fortune of the carers' story.

Postscript
Still an open book

As, so to speak, the ink was drying on the last page of this history there was published in January 2007 a report from the Commission for Social Care Inspection. The report anticipated a forthcoming crisis in the care of the elderly. There is around the corner a crisis in care services reflecting the growing longevity of disabled people, often with high support needs, as well as the growing elderly population. Demographics indicated that by 2028 there will be 1.8 million people over the age of 85.

The care system is already beginning to crack under the strain. The majority of local authorities, for example, now limit home care to people with needs assessed as 'critical' or 'substantial'. These criteria will only tighten in the years ahead. There are variable hourly charges for local authority home care, with the most expensive authority charging three times as much as the cheapest. Local authorities are clearly having to ration their services by targeting the most needy. But as budgets become tighter the cut off point for 'most needy' is inevitably drawn more and more narrowly. Carers now are beginning to experience these cut-backs in, for example, a week's reduction in respite care.

For Carers UK and all carer-based organisations, 2007 has begun with a stark challenge. The history of the movement shows it is capable of rising to this challenge, but how it does so and what will be involved will have to be the subject of a subsequent history.

Tim Cook
11 January 2007

SOURCES

In agreement with Carers UK I have not referenced this history as one might a more academic work. Most of the publications to which reference is made have been cited clearly in the text itself. As indicated in the Acknowledgements at the front of this book, much of the internal documentation up to 1999 is in the G/CA Records of the Carer's Association in the Greater Manchester County Record Office, with the Catalogue of Archives running to 229 pages.

Other sources which have been valuable and which are not cited fully in the text are given below.

Madeleine Bunting, *Willing Slaves*, Harper Perennial, 2004

Helene Curtis and Mimi Sanderson, *The Unsung Sixties*, Whiting and Birch, 2004

Jim Orford et al, *Coping with Alcohol and Drug Problems*, Routledge, 2005

Jill Pitkeathley, *It's My Duty, Isn't It?* Souvenir Press, 1989

Pat Thane, *Old Age in English History*, OUP, 2000. This is essential reading for any historical understanding of caring in families and the section on Before Recognition in this account owes everything to Pat Thane's work. All my historical references such as Elizabeth Robert's work can be found in Thane.

Nicholas Timms, *The Five Giants, A Biography of the Welfare State*, Fontana, 1996

How devolution has impacted on the carers' movement: the Scottish case study

Devolution was intended to promote a new partnership between citizens and the Scottish Parliament. It provided unique opportunities for carers and carer organisations to work directly with the Scottish Executive, MSPs and civil servants. Carers Scotland has been able to work closely with Ministers responsible for carers' issues, Executive officials in the Carers Branch and with individual MSPs. Additionally, since devolution Carers Scotland and the national carer organisations have supported the work of a Parliamentary Cross Party Group on Carers (originally established to facilitate work on the Community Care & Health (Scotland) Act 2002 and re-established to support the recommendations of the Care 21 report (see 'legislation and policy' below).

Carers Scotland has been involved in shaping a range of policy initiatives and legislative developments. These have included an ongoing commitment to the development and implementation of legislation, including the Adults with Incapacity (Scotland) Act 2000, the Community Care & Health (Scotland) Act 2002 and the Mental Health (Care & Treatment) (Scotland) Act 2003 and, to policy initiatives such as Building a Health Service Fit for the Future (see 'Carers and Health' below), the Joint Futures agenda (see 'Promoting

Carer Involvement' below) and Changing Lives, a new initiative to support major changes in how social work services are planned and delivered.

In seeking to effect significant changes in carers' lives, Carers Scotland has focused its campaigning and development work around three key themes:

EQUALITY

Carers should not have to suffer poverty or social exclusion as a result of their caring role. They have the same right as everyone else to public services, a social life, and access to the world of work and education.

EMPOWERMENT

Campaigning for carer equality is about empowering carers to speak up for themselves, promoting access to personal learning and development and ensuring carers are a much more visible group in society.

PARTNERSHIP

Carers were designated in legislation as 'key partners in the provision of care'. Carers Scotland works to make this more of a reality, by promoting partnership working between the voluntary sector, government, health and social work authorities and, most importantly, carers themselves.

Under the auspices of these overarching themes work has developed in four key areas:

- Legislation and policy
- Promoting carer involvement

- Promoting carers' health
- Promoting carers' employment and lifelong learning opportunities.

LEGISLATION AND POLICY

COMMUNITY CARE & HEALTH (SCOTLAND) ACT 2002

In September 2002, new legal rights in the form of the Community Care and Health (Scotland) Act 2002 recognised the contribution of many thousands of unpaid carers in Scotland. Carers Scotland supported carers' involvement in developing this legislation. Carers were involved in drafting guidance, strategic planning, lobbying, consultation, giving evidence and working with Members of the Scottish Parliament. Carers Scotland sought to facilitate as much direct involvement of carers with Ministers and MSPs as possible.

The involvement of carers in the policy process was a positive one. Both carers and carers' organisations had a favourable impression of the Scottish Parliament and MSPs. Many carers commented that they did not expect to be so well received and felt that their opinions had been truly valued. The Health and Community Care Committee of the Scottish Parliament was praised by the carer representative who felt that they treated her as having an expert opinion.

The Community Care and Health (Scotland) Act 2002 provides evidence that the civil servants, Members of the Scottish Parliament, Scottish Ministers, carer organisations and carers have embraced the opportunities presented by devolution to increase access to the policy process by individual citizens. Being involved in the policy process was seen as positive by all and is an example of the benefits of an inclusive approach to legislative development.

CARE 21: THE FUTURE OF UNPAID CARE IN SCOTLAND

Carers Scotland, carers, national and local carer organisations have been fully involved in the development of the report 'Care 21: the future of unpaid care in Scotland'. The project is the first of its kind in Europe and the report has major significance for carers in Scotland and for the future of unpaid caring.

The report reflects the views of carers, with several thousand carers taking part in surveys to inform the research for the report and many also taking part in interviews, focus and stakeholder groups.

The report's recommendations are not just for the Scottish Executive but also for the UK Government, statutory and voluntary sectors. It projects a bold vision for carers in Scotland – based on a strong framework of rights – where the caring contribution of carers to society is fully recognised, the economic impact of their contribution accepted and where carers are fully included in a society which will provide adequate support to carers.

The Scottish Executive published its response to the report following several months of scoping the implications and potential of each recommendation. This process also involved Carers Scotland and the national carer organisations in Scotland.

There has been acceptance of most of the recommendations and the Executive has made a commitment to a 10 year programme of action to support carers in Scotland. Unfortunately, at this point, no additional resources are available. However, work is underway to assess resource implications in a number of areas to inform the Spending Review in 2007.

Carers' organisations, including Carers Scotland, continue to lobby MSPs to ensure broad support for carers in this Spending Review. Since the report's publication, a petition has been presented to the Public Petitions Committee and carer organisations held a reception for carers and MSPs, hosted by John Swinney MSP. The Petitions Committee have asked the Parliament's Health Committee to monitor the implementation of Care 21 recommendations and seek further evidence on the capacity, expansion and costs of delivery.

In addition, during Carers Week, Carers Scotland's Action for Carers and Employment initiative organised a reception for carers and MSPs hosted by Cathy Peattie MSP. This followed a Parliamentary debate on a motion in support of carers (again by Cathy Peattie MSP), which received broad support, with a number of MSPs taking part and more than 60% supporting the motion itself.

This work will continue alongside activities to ensure that the support of carers is maintained and developed with each of the parties and their candidates in the 2007 Scottish Parliamentary election.

Carers Scotland and other national carer organisations continue to work with the Scottish Executive (including meeting with the Deputy Minister for Health and Community Care on a quarterly basis) to support developments for the four early priority areas – respite, carers' health, carer training and young carers. This includes working on the two Executive task groups on respite and young carers and providing evidence for additional resources in the Spending Review.

PROMOTING CARER INVOLVEMENT

JOINT FUTURE FOR CARERS

This project was a partnership initiative between Carers Scotland and the Coalition of Carers in Scotland, funded by the Scottish Executive. The project aimed to improve the level of involvement of carers in local community care planning and to ensure that, as key partners in the provision of care, carers' involvement is meaningful and effective.

A survey and consultation exercise was undertaken to assess the extent to which carers are actively involved in local planning processes, and the level of consultation with carers in devising community care packages.

The recommendations and action points were taken forward and developed into an action learning programme aimed at developing skills amongst local carers groups and representatives from statutory service planning and provider agencies in local government and the NHS.

CARERS' INVOLVEMENT IN THE INSPECTION PROCESS

Carers Scotland worked with the new Social Work Inspection Agency to involve carers in social work inspections of social work services across Scotland. A number of carers have been involved and Carers Scotland is now working with Social Work Inspection Agency to develop a training framework for carer involvement in inspection programmes.

PROMOTING CARERS HEALTH

Carers Scotland was instrumental in bringing the work of the researcher Michael Hirst on the health needs of carers onto the Scottish political agenda. Initiated by a major conference in 2004, 'Carers Health: Working for a Positive Future' highlighted that the stress of caring can affect the physical and mental health of carers and that a range of measures including practical support, information, occupational health measures and the introduction of carers' health needs into public health agendas, can bring significant benefits and stop today's carers becoming tomorrow's patients. Carers Scotland continued to build on this message and worked with those developing 'Building a Health Service Fit for the Future' (known as the Kerr Report) to introduce carers' health needs to the wider NHS agenda including the development of NHS Carer Information Strategies, expert carer training for carers and the introduction of GP carer registers.

PROMOTING CARERS EMPLOYMENT AND LIFELONG LEARNING OPPORTUNITIES

CARERS AND EMPLOYMENT

In a significant partnership with the Equal Opportunities Commission and the Association of Directors of Social Work, Carers Scotland has developed the Action for Carers and Employment initiative in Scotland. The initiative is working to promote flexible working for carers and the provision of flexible alternative carer services to enable carers to remain in or enter employment. A conference on Flexible Working for employers was held in February 2006 followed by the establishment of a stakeholder group to develop a framework for flexible working. Alongside this, two local authorities are developing best practice in holistic carers' assessments and in the provision of Direct Payments.

LEARNING FOR LIVING

Carers Scotland in partnership with City and Guilds has developed a personal development and learning tool for carers called 'Learning for Living'. Learning for Living consists of online learning resources for carers and a qualification.

The Certificate in Personal Development and Learning for Unpaid Carers aims to give carers the confidence and support they may need to achieve their personal goals. It also seeks to acknowledge and validate the skills carers develop as carers. This is the first qualification of its kind specifically designed to help unpaid carers back into paid employment or on to further training.

The first learners to complete the course received their certificates in 2006. So far over 140 carers have commenced the course. It is hoped that carers across Scotland will have access to the programme.

CONTRIBUTION TO CARERS UK DEVELOPMENTS

Working as a devolved entity that remains an integral part of Carers UK has been an exciting journey for all of the nations. However it has been a productive and mutually beneficial process. The Directors actively support the Chief Executive in shaping strategic direction and developments and in managing the key activities. It is generally acknowledged that being part of a UK organisation brings added value to both.

LOOKING TO THE FUTURE

The Scottish Executive has set out an ambitious ten-year plan for carers. There will be many challenges in seeking to implement the carers' agenda, not least the major challenge of securing funding to continue to campaign for carers' rights. Carers Scotland is committed to pursuing this agenda as part of Carers UK.